IPSWICH TOWN

A HISTORY

IPSWICH TOWN

A HISTORY

SUSAN GARDINER

AMBERLEY

First published 2013

Amberley Publishing
The Hill, Stroud
Gloucestershire, GL5 4EP

www.amberley-books.com

British Library Cataloguing in Publication Data.
A catalogue record for this book is available from the British Library.

ISBN 978 1 4456 1723 7 (print)
ISBN 978 1 4456 1735 0 (ebook)

Typeset in 10pt on 12pt Sabon.
Typesetting and Origination by Amberley Publishing.
Printed in the UK.

Contents

Foreword by James Scowcroft

I'll always remember my first time on the Portman Road pitch.

It was back in April 1989 and I'd just finished my Centre of Excellence training in the old indoor gymnasium, which was the idea of Sir Bobby Robson. Football on the pitch had taken a back seat that week, as it was only three days after the Hillsborough tragedy. At the North Stand end, there were a couple of bunches of flowers and some Ipswich and Liverpool scarves tied to the goal nets. Nobody was about, so I strolled onto the pitch and went over to see what had been left and read the condolences that had been written.

On the way back, I stopped in the centre circle and looked up at the impressive three-tiered Pioneer Stand. I was only thirteen at the time but allowed myself to dream about what it would be like to play at Portman Road in a first-team game. Six years later, I was lucky enough to find that my ambition had come true.

I went on to have six years playing for the club. A club that has a history and identity second to none. A club that has produced two of the greatest managers England have ever seen, won domestic and European honours only other clubs can dream of, produced home grown players that have gone on to represent their country with pride, but most of all a football club that has had wonderful links with it's local community and supporters.

I'm pleased to introduce this new history of Ipswich Town and the people who made it one of the most successful and famous football clubs in the world.

Introduction

'A Town Consecrated to Football'

On 12 January 1939, *The Times* reported on a match played at Portman Road between Ipswich Town Football Club, a team that had just been elected to the Third Division of the Football League, and Aston Villa, who were then a well-established side having already won the FA Cup six times. The match at Ipswich was a replay in the third round of the FA Cup and Town lost by two goals to one, but the next day, *The Times* reporter praised the team's football skills, saying that they had 'every right to consider themselves unfortunate'. He also spoke highly of the quality of the playing surface at Portman Road and went on to say:

> Ipswich as a town seemed yesterday consecrated to football, and long before noon there were long queues outside the ground and the crowd was a record one. The game rewarded the patience of the thousands who stood and waited.

There have been several excellent histories of Ipswich Town to date, including a magnificently comprehensive book by the late John Eastwood and Tony Moyse, *The Men Who Made The Town*, which was published in 1986. I have drawn upon it, and the website based on it, Pride of Anglia, heavily as a resource for facts and statistics and I am extremely grateful to its authors. I have, however, attempted to write a very different book examining the relationship between the football club and the town through various themes, such as work, war, identity and some of the many different people who have made the club what it is today.

It has been more than a decade since Ipswich Town were in the top tier of English football, but it still holds a central place in the heart of the town and in the hearts of its supporters. We still look forward – stupidly, blindly, romantically, perhaps – to the time when the club will be restored to its rightful place among the brightest and the best of football teams.

Football clubs may have become big business in the modern era, but a football club is fundamentally made up of people: the players, the staff and the supporters. In fact, it took decades to persuade Ipswich Town's founding fathers that the club should be anything other than a purely amateur sports organisation. The idea that it should have become a multi-million pound enterprise with supporters' groups all around the world would have seemed both laughable and slightly offensive to the men and women who did 'make the Town'.

All football supporters feel that their club is unique and has a special place in the history of the game. This may be particularly true for Ipswich Town fans. We have often been accused of living in the past but have, at least, a substantial and fascinating past in which to live. The events of the 1938/39 season, when Ipswich Town joined the Football League, were the first steps – soon interrupted by a World War – on the way to becoming First Division championship winners (1961/62), FA Cup winners (1978) and UEFA Cup winners (1981) under two of the greatest managers ever to work in English football, Sir Alf Ramsey and Sir Bobby Robson. Most people would agree that is a history worth having.

Acknowledgements

I am particularly grateful to Pat Godbold for giving me her valuable time and knowledge of the club's history, and also the privilege of meeting a lady who, in many ways, epitomises all that is best about Ipswich Town.

I would also like to thank Len Fletcher and his lovely wife, who were kind enough to invite me to their home and tell me so much about the club and its staff in the immediate post-war period.

The following people helped and supported me while I wrote this book. I would not have been able to write it without them: Che Barber, Gavin Barber, Andrew Barnard, Emma Corlett, Joe Fairs, Kingsley Fletcher, Dave Gooderham, David Kindred, Colin Kreidewolf, Matt Makin, Alasdair Ross, David Jameson, Simone Longo, James Scowcroft and Seàn Salter.

I am also grateful to my editor at Amberley Publishing, Tom Furby, and the staff of the Suffolk Library Service, Ipswich Record Office, Norfolk Library Service and A. E. Coe Ltd.

1

The Beginnings of Football in East Anglia

Football has probably been played in England since Roman times, and perhaps long before that. For centuries, those in government regarded it with mistrust, and steps were periodically taken to control and even ban it. Its origins were in rough and often very violent games that were more like mass brawls. The traditional Shrove Tuesday match at Ashbourne in Derbyshire is probably the last remaining example of what this kind of football was like. Serious injuries and even deaths sometimes occurred, such was the violence of the game. It was played between two groups of villagers over a large area; a 'goal' could be in a different parish from where the game had started. Because of the disorder associated with these games, football was unpopular with the ruling authorities from medieval times onwards and laws were constantly being passed to ban or regulate it on the grounds, for example, that it distracted young men from archery practice. Archers were required to fight for their country in time of war; football was not thought to be so useful to society.

During times of hardship, these games would sometimes end in food riots or protests against the forced enclosure of common land. Such a riot took place in Kettering, Northamptonshire in 1765. In towns, impromptu games of street football by apprentices (who were always up for a riot) often ended in violence and damage to property. In 1835, the Highways Act prohibited the playing of football on the highway, with stiff fines for anyone who was caught. Because of its prohibition, combined with the long working hours of those who worked on the land or in factories, opportunities for the labouring classes to play the game were reduced. Nevertheless, this crude form of football continued to be played up to the middle of the nineteenth century.

East Anglia had its own special form of football, known as *camp-ball* or *camping*. Several sites of former 'camping closes' have been located in

Suffolk, as well as in Norfolk and Cambridgeshire. If you look out of the window of a train going through Needham Market, for example, you can still see the site of the camping field where this very rough form of the game was played. In *Popular Recreations in English Society 1700–1850*, Robert W. Malcolmson mentions camping closes or football fields at Needham, Buxhall, Fressingfield, Ashfield and Harleston in Suffolk.

Suffolk poet Thomas Tusser mentions the game in his *Five Hundreth Pointes of Good Husbandrie*, written in 1573, even recommending its positive effects on the land:

> In meadow or pasture (to grow the more fine)
> Let campers be camping in any of thine;
> Which if ye do suffer, when low is the spring,
> You gain to yourself a commodious thing.

There was also a football ground at Hawstead, according to Sir John Cullum, who in his *History and Antiquities of Hawsted in the County of Suffolk* (1784) wrote about a fifteenth-century document in which:

> mention is made of the *camping pightel*, which joined to the east-side of the church-yard. The field has entirely lost its name, which is the more remarkable, as in some parts this active game of our ancestors is still much in fashion ... If any such existed here, as from the name there probably did, the plough has levelled them, as in other places, and the very tradition of the sport is forgotten.

It is difficult to believe that informal games of football disappeared from the Suffolk countryside or its towns altogether during this period, and its revival in the nineteenth century indicates that it was still played in some form.

2

Origins

Despite the general disapproval of football when played by labourers, by the mid-nineteenth century many public schoolboys had taken the game up enthusiastically. The pupils may have been from the upper classes, but some of their masters were from less privileged backgrounds, and these teachers may have introduced what was traditionally a labouring-class game to the young gentlemen of Eton and Shrewsbury. Whatever the explanation, several rough forms of football were being played in English public schools by the time the Football Association was formed 150 years ago.

Public schools at that time were violent and even cruel places. Partly in an attempt to regulate the barbarity in these schools, the reformers of the Victorian era attempted to codify the two games of rugby and association football. As we shall see, it is no coincidence that several of the founder members of Ipswich Association Football Club were former pupils of Ipswich School.

In his history of association football, *The People's Game*, James Walvin suggests that the popularity of football in East Anglia may have been one of the reasons that it became established 'as an undergraduate recreation in its own right' at Cambridge University. Although the game had been banned for long periods at both Oxford and Cambridge universities, former public schoolboys at Cambridge became organised to the extent that they drafted what came to be known as the 'Cambridge Rules'; these formed the basis of the Football Association code drawn up in 1863, which still governs the game today.

The enthusiasm of these public school-educated graduates for the game of association football continued throughout their lives and, combined with the movement known as 'muscular Christianity', which was also influential in the mid-nineteenth century, led to many of those who were interested in social issues to take a different view of sport, and of football in particular. Rather than seeing it as a barbarous and potentially disruptive activity, the new approach regarded athleticism and masculinity as desirable attributes. Many reformers who came into regular contact with the poor believed that the encouragement of young men to participate in football was a force for good. The philosophy was 'a healthy mind in a healthy body', and sport was seen by many reformers as a good way to improve the general health of the population, as well as to distract the working man away from the heavy drinking, gambling and blood sports that often occupied his very limited leisure hours.

Ironically, having spent centuries trying to suppress and control football among the poor, the late nineteenth century saw the upper classes using the codified game as a way of 'improving' them.

Ipswich in 1878

In the year that its association football club was founded Ipswich was a very different town to the place we know today. Men wore bowler or 'stove pipe' hats, and the bustle had recently replaced the crinoline as the latest in women's fashion. Travel around town was by coach or cart, although most people travelled on foot, even for very long distances. Ipswich's horse tramway was not built until 1879. The telephone was invented in 1876, but was not in general use until much later. Communication was by word of mouth or local newspapers. The well-established *Ipswich Journal* covered national and county news, as did *The East Anglian Daily Times,* which was first published in 1874.

In 1878, the first public electric lights were installed in London. It was not long before the first floodlit football match was played at Bramall Lane, Sheffield, in October, two days before the inaugural meeting of Ipswich Association Football Club. Rather impressively, Ipswich itself played a football match under electric light at the Orwell Works ground, Brook's Hall, December 1878. Confusingly, the match was advertised under the auspices of Ipswich (Rugby) Football Club, but the newspaper report of the match between 'Ipswich' and a 'United Suffolk' side lists players better-known for the association game, including George Sherrington and J. H. Knights, who scored two out of the five goals. It may well be that, as Henderson and Voller suggest in their history of the club, *The Essential History of Ipswich Town,* published in 2001, that a combination of the two codes was played.

In Ipswich, the Medical Officer for Health reported several cases of smallpox, as well as typhoid fever, measles, whooping cough, scarlet fever and diarrhoea. There was a 'excessive number of deaths' among children in St Clement's parish, which was the poorest part of Ipswich:

The majority of the premises visited where the deaths took place were found to be in a bad sanitary state, and infectious diseases appear to be more prevalent in those districts where the drainage was defective.

He went on to describe the River Gipping as being in a 'foul state' and 'little better than an open sewer'.

In February 1878, the Ipswich Board of Guardians reported that they had given out relief to 575 persons in the previous year, and debated whether or not to improve conditions in the infirmary of the Workhouse on Great Whip Street. One of the guardians, a Mr Fisk, objected to the suggestion of more comfortable beds in the infirmary, adding that 'wire beds are luxuries which people can have if they like to pay for them'. In October, the *Ipswich Journal* reported that the Board of Guardians had assisted 460 'outdoor paupers', 192 inside the workhouse and 67 homeless people.

Opportunities for recreation among the working classes were increasing but there was not a great deal to do in Ipswich, apart from some rather worthy entertainments put on by well-meaning people. In 1850, John Glyde, in his book *The Moral, Social and Religious History of Ipswich in the Middle of the Nineteenth Century*, listed the following institutions as being suitable for 'improving and refining the mind' of local young men: Ipswich Public Library, the Literary Institution, the Mechanics' Institute, the Young Men's Association, the Mental Improvement Society, the Philological Society, Ipswich Museum, the Philosophical Society, the Microscopical Society and the Fine Arts Association.

The social highlights of the year 1876 were, it seems, the opening of a skating rink and a Spelling Bee held at Ipswich Town Hall. On the other hand, *Kelly's Post Office Directory of Suffolk for 1865* listed 186 public houses, inns and hotels in the Ipswich area. The social reformers, who were determined to clamp down on the consumption of alcohol among working-class men in Ipswich, clearly had their work cut out.

The Foundation of Ipswich Association Football Club

It was in this context that Ipswich Association Football Club was founded in October 1878. The *East Anglian Daily Times* reported the first meeting, which took place on 16 October, in the following day's edition:

NEW CLUB IN IPSWICH. A meeting, convened by circular, was held at the Town Hall, on Wednesday evening, for the purpose of forming a football club, playing under Association rules. A large number of gentlemen were present, amongst whom we noticed the following: F. G. Bond, G. S. Sherrington, J. M. Franks, E. Turner, A. S. Bond,

J. H. H. Knights, G. K. Smith, F. Prentice, W. Fiske, A. Edwards, W. Smythe, S. King, &c., &c. Mr T. C. Cobbold, M.P., was unanimously voted president, subject to his consent. The post of captain was deferred for further consideration. Mr J. H. H. Knights was elected honorary secretary; and the following on the committee:- Messrs. F. G. Bond, 13 votes; J. M. Franks, 13; G. S. Sherrington, 11; C. Fisher, 5. The first game was fixed for Saturday week, on the club ground, at Broom Hill, Norwich Road, at three p.m. The club will be called the Ipswich Association Football Club, and will, as above stated, play under the rules sanctioned by the association. This will be rather a novelty to the Ipswich public, who have been used to the very different play of the Ipswich club under the Rugby rules. Without giving an opinion on the relative merits of the two systems, we may express our pleasure that the young men of the town have resolved to afford themselves and the public a taste of the original style of football. There is plenty of room in the town for both clubs and we hope that the young one will not fail through want of support – much less from jealousy – from the direction of Portman's [*sic*] Road.

This short report gives several interesting insights into the background of the club's foundation. The suggestion that there might be rivalry or even 'jealousy' between the two codes of rugby and association football reveals something about the history of the two games in Ipswich. For many years – until 1888, in fact – the football played at Portman Road was rugby, but the association game was increasing in popularity, both as a sport to participate in and to watch from the touchline. It is probably unwise to overstate that rivalry, however. The players of both forms of the game came from the same social circle in Ipswich and would have known each other well. Often the same names – Sherrington, Turner, Peecock – crop up in rugby and association match reports, either because some footballers played both codes or their brothers did.

A report of an early friendly between Ipswich Association Football Club and another local side, Stoke Wanderers, in the *Ipswich Journal* on Saturday 2 November 1878, gives a taste of what those early matches were like:

The match was played on Saturday last, 2 November, on the ground of the former, Broom Hill, Norwich Road. The Wanderers not being an Association club played under the disadvantage of not knowing the rules, and although possessing greater speed than their opponents, they were out-matched from the first, and when time was called the Association club was victorious by six goals (Knights four and H. Peecock two) to one. Great praise is due to the Wanderers for the plucky and good tempered manner in which they played a losing game. For the victors the goal keeping of Herring was worthy of notice, as was also the play of Hamby at 'side', and for the Wanderers, Snelling, Hughes and Catchpole were most conspicuous.

Ipswich School

Football seems to have been played informally at Ipswich School from the 1850s onwards. A history of the school (Gray & Potter's *Ipswich School, 1400–1950*) describes the early days:

> Football was played whenever possible. No general code of rules existed in the fifties ... any neighbouring club sides that existed drawing their players for the most part from the old boys of local [i.e. private] schools ... Since, however, no two schools had exactly the same rules, inter-school matches were rare and outside fixtures were usually against teams of old-boys ... At Ipswich pick-up games took place on half-holidays; usually all boys who were interested turned up and games were arranged with complete disregard for size, sometimes twenty-five to thirty boys playing on a side.

Gray and Potter's school history includes a list of the captains of school and the various sports teams. Football captains are listed from 1866 and, starting with William Sherrington in 1877, the list includes a number of boys who would go on to play for Ipswich AFC: G. S. Sherrington (1878/79), F. C. Peecock (1880), F. W. Turner (1886), A. E. Harrison (1889), C. L. Alexander (1890), F. H. Alexander (1891), J. R. Cornell (1898), C. Palmer (1899/1900), H. Prankerd (1901), W. H. Dunnett (1905), and H. F. R. Miller (1918/19). K. F. Marks appears to be the last Ipswich School football captain (1922/23) to go on to play for Ipswich, and the decreasing frequency of this transition from school footballer to the town side reflects a gradual change, as players from a wider range of social backgrounds were recruited to play, even for the amateur side.

At a meeting of Ipswich Association Football Club at the Great White Horse Hotel in Tavern Street at the end of the 1886/87 season, William Sherrington said that Ipswich School 'might fairly be called the nursery of Suffolk football. For the last few years it has produced certainly the majority of the players for the county, and the greater part for the more prominent clubs.'

Founder Members and Early Players

Who were the people who were present at that first meeting of Ipswich Association Football Club?

Thomas Clement Cobbold (1833–83)

The first president, elected unanimously at the 16 October 1878 meeting, was Thomas Clement Cobbold, who was also the Member of Parliament for Ipswich for the entire time of his involvement with the football club. He had been a scholar at Ipswich School and had also played football at Charterhouse, one of the top public schools in England. The club's first match – a friendly – was between the Secretary's Team and The Club (a 2-2 draw). T. C. Cobbold presented the ball, kicked off and played, reportedly 'with great spirit'.

His obituary in *The Times*, Thursday 22 November 1883, sums up the facts of his life:

> The Press Association states that Mr Thomas Clement Cobbold, MP for Ipswich, died last night at a quarter to 9. The deceased was the third son of the late John Chevallier Cobbold, of the Holywells, Suffolk, who represented Ipswich from 1847 to 1868, by Lucy, the third daughter of the Rev. Henry Patteson, of Drinkstone, Suffolk. The deceased was the brother of the late John Patteson Cobbold, who sat for Ipswich from February, 1874, till his death in December, 1875. Mr T. C. Cobbold was born at Ipswich in 1833, and was educated at the Charterhouse. He entered the diplomatic service ... in 1854 ... He was a Conservative, who was inclined to support and encourage every well-considered measure for progress. He had sat for Ipswich since December, 1875.

T. C. Cobbold was president of the football club between 1878 and 1883. A diplomat with little previous involvement in football, he was the first of a long line of members of the local brewing dynasty to take a leading role at the club and set a pattern of public school-educated, politically Conservative, patrician chairmen that was uninterrupted until the club was acquired by Marcus Evans in 2007.

G. S. Sherrington (1861–1942)

George Stuart Sherrington was born in Islington on 20 August 1861 and was baptised there, along with his older brother, William Stainton Sherrington, who was also a talented sportsman. As well as being a founder of Ipswich Association Football Club at the same time, G. S. Sherrington was captain of the Ipswich School football team from 1878 to 1879, his brother William having been captain in 1877.

George and William Sherrington, along with their older brother, Charles, were almost certainly the illegitimate sons of Anne Brookes, *née* Thurtell and Caleb Rose, a leading surgeon from Ipswich, with whom she was living in College Road, Islington in London at the time that all three boys were born. No father was named in the baptism register of St James' church, Clerkenwell, and there is no official record of the registration of any of their births. It was claimed they were the sons of a country doctor, James Norton Sherrington. However, it was with Caleb Rose that Anne and the three Sherrington boys moved to Anglesea Road, Ipswich in 1860 and the couple were married in 1880 after Caleb's first wife had died. They were an intellectual and athletic family, important to Ipswich School and to the founding of Ipswich Association Football Club. As adults, George and William became successful solicitors in the town and Charles, who was also a keen footballer and all-round sportsman, won the Nobel Prize for Medicine in 1932.

George Sherrington was only seventeen years old and a pupil at Ipswich School when he first played for Ipswich. He was still playing football for Ipswich in 1889, and was involved in football for much longer as an administrator. He served for many years on several Suffolk County Football Association and national Football Association committees. A further important link between the Sherrington family and Ipswich Association Football Club is that of Broom Hill Park, which was the site of the first-ever game the Association played, the land that Ipswich played on was owned by the Sherrington family.

J. H. H. Knights (1859–94)

John Hopkins Horsburgh Knights was the son of George Knights, who was the curator of Ipswich Museum for eighteen years. Born at Whitton, then a village near Ipswich, on 9 February 1859, John lived with his father in the town until his early death in 1874. John was only fourteen years old when his father died. He was a Queen's Scholar at Ipswich School, and so was gifted intellectually as well as athletically. His name frequently appeared in newspaper reports of the school sports days of the time. He played for Ipswich Association Football Club for many years, often captaining the side. In 1881, he was living with his widowed mother, a lodging-house keeper and working as an insurance clerk. He died very young, aged only thirty-five, of phthisis (probably caused by tuberculosis) in Felixstowe where he had gone in an effort to recuperate. His obituary appeared in the *Ipswich Journal* on 30 June 1894:

DEATH OF MR JOHN KNIGHTS – It is with much regret that we record the death of Mr John H. Knights, of Handford Villas, Ipswich, which sad event took place on Thursday morning at Felixstowe, where he had been staying in the hope of recruiting (*sic*) his health, which has for some time been declining. A year since Mr Knights undertook a voyage to Australia, trusting that beneficial results might follow, but, as is now known, the good results so ardently wished for were not, unhappily, realised. Mr Knights was the only son of the late Mr George Knights (Curator of the Ipswich Museum) and of Mrs Waugh, Meynell House, Newmarket, and was 35 years of age. For the greater part of his life he was connected with the Alliance Insurance Company at Ipswich, and at the time of his lamented death held a responsible position in their office. Always courteous and obliging, he gained many friends, who will greatly deplore their loss. In sports he always took a keen interest, and will be remembered as the popular captain and centre-forward in the now defunct Ipswich Association Football Club, which in years gone by fought out many a battle on Broom Hill. Mr Knights leaves a widow (a daughter of the late Mr Alfred Edwards, of Westgate Street) and three children.

The reference to Ipswich Association Football Club being 'defunct' was because in September 1888, it had been decided that it should amalgamate with Ipswich Football Club (the rugby club) and become Ipswich Town Football Club. Matches from then on would be played at Portman Road.

J. M. Franks (1854–1941)

Franks does not appear to have been a pupil at Ipswich School. He was born in Harwich, Essex, in 1854, the son of a banker's clerk and coal merchant who had himself been born in Ipswich. At the age of sixteen, he was living with his grandfather, a schoolmaster, in Elm Street, Ipswich. His grandfather was James Franks, a stalwart of the local community, involved in several insurance schemes, a member of the St Mary Elms parish council and a Freemason. He was also on the committee for the election of John Chevallier Cobbold to Parliament and, it would appear from his presence at many meetings at least, he was a leading member of the Ipswich Conservative Party. It isn't difficult to see that the young James Maurice Franks, bank clerk, would have moved in some of the same circles as his teammates at Ipswich Association Football Club, even if he hadn't attended Ipswich School.

As a footballer, Franks was praised for his skills in 'dribbling' the ball. He was often picked out in match reports as 'conspicuous' and was a regular goalscorer. At the first meeting of the Association he was elected chairman of the club remarking that:

An Association Club was quite a novelty in Ipswich, but I think that anyone who has played that game would consider it worth playing occasionally. I hope that no one will consider that the promoters have any antagonistic feelings with regard to the Ipswich [i.e. rugby] Club, but that the two clubs might prosper, both being of mutual assistance to the other. (*Ipswich Journal*, 22 October 1878)

He served as club secretary for the 1880/81 season. In 1901, he was living as a very respectable member of society in Hampden in Arden, Warwickshire, but by 1911, he had moved to Surrey and died there in 1941.

F. G. Bond (1861–1920) and A. S. Bond (b. 1863)
Frederic George Bond and Arthur Simpson Bond were the sons of a land agent. Frederic was born in Ipswich in 1861, when his family were living in Tavern Street. His brother was born three years later in December 1863. They both followed in their father's footsteps and became auctioneers and land agents.

Henry Bunnell Burton (c. 1859–1943)
Burton was the son of a grocer from Neale Street, Ipswich. In the 1881 census, he is described as a 'merchant importer' and in 1891 as a 'sugar merchant and miller'. He went to Ipswich School and was later chairman of the school's governors. He was Ipswich's first ever goalscorer in a 2-0 victory away at Harwich on 9 November 1878. Later, he became chairman of the Ipswich firm Burton, Son & Saunders. In 1910, he stood as the losing candidate in a general election for the Unionist Party. His son was killed in the First World War and a grandson of his became head of the famous Suffolk firm of Fisons. He was knighted in 1934.

S. A. Notcutt (1865–1923)
Stephen Abbott Notcutt played for Ipswich at right-back between 1885 and 1893. He was one of five generations with the same name: when the first Stephen Notcutt married into the wealthy Abbott family, it was stipulated as a condition of the marriage that the Abbott family fortune would continue to be left to the eldest son only for as long as he used the name Abbott. His grandfather, Stephen Abbott Notcutt who was a Unitarian attorney and very active in Ipswich political life, had been town clerk and was elected as a Portman. Other members of the Notcutt family served on the Board of Guardians that ran the workhouse. His brother, Richard Crompton Notcutt, began the well-known horticultural company of the same name in 1897.

Another all-round athlete who played football and cricket for the Suffolk county side, Stephen Notcutt was a pupil at Ipswich School – in the early

1880s he was playing for both the school team and Ipswich AFC – and he became an important figure in the relationship between the school, the 'Old Ipswichians' (the former pupils' society) and county sport, including association football. Growing up in Anglesea Road, Ipswich, it is not too fanciful to imagine that he was quite close to the Sherrington brothers, who went to the same school, university and also practised as solicitors in the town. After graduating from St John's College, Cambridge in 1883, Stephen became a solicitor in the family firm – his father, a solicitor of the same name had died in 1875. Along with the Sherringtons, he was one of the prime movers in the eventual amalgamation of Ipswich Association Football Club with the rugby club and the move to Portman Road.

Notcutt was in the Suffolk County side against Preston North End at Portman Road on 24 March 1892, the first match against a professional team played there. He unsuccessfully attempted, as club president, to have a grandstand constructed at Portman Road as early as 1892. As the definitive club history *The Men Who Made the Town* says of him, 'The initiative displayed ... was typical of the man, he certainly contributed much to the early development of Ipswich Town.'

Notcutt's playing career was cut short in 1893 following an injury to a tendon in his left leg, but he continued to serve the interests of football in the town for many years – as late as December 1898, the *Ipswich Journal* reported that he represented Ipswich at a meeting of the Suffolk County Football Association at the Station Hotel in the town. He continued his involvement with the club until his death in December 1923.

Ernest Aldous Kent (1863–1960)

Also known as 'Toby', he was born at Little Bealings in 1863, the son of Francis and Mary Kent. His father was a teacher at the national school in Bealings but later moved with his large family to Kesgrave, near Ipswich, where he became headmaster of Kesgrave Hall School. Ernest was a pupil there between 1881 and 1885. He was apprenticed at Cowell's, the Ipswich printers and later worked in that trade in Kingston, Surrey (around 1881). He returned to live in Ipswich in about 1901. By 1911, however, he was living along with his Surrey-born wife, Rosalie and their five-year-old daughter, Katharine in Worsley, Lancashire and was clerk to a colliery. He died at the age of ninety-two, having returned to live with his daughter back in Finningham, Suffolk in June 1960. He was an important figure in the early history of Ipswich Town and was the first player ever to have a testimonial match played for him. His ashes were scattered at Portman Road.

He made his debut for Ipswich in the 1887/88 season, but was forced to retire through injury in 1902. Playing as an insid-forward or centre-forward, he scored fifty-five goals in competitive games. He wrote several articles about the early days of football in the *Ipswich Star*, extracts from which are transcribed below.

F. C. Peecock (1864–1920)

Francis Charles Peecock, the son of a commercial traveller in the iron industry and originally from Great Blakenham in Suffolk, was captain of the Ipswich School football team in 1880. He was yet another Ipswich School boy who went on to be an important figure in the early development of Ipswich Town.

There were six Peecock brothers and five of them, Francis, John, Edwin, Henry, and Robert, all played for the club and several of them also played for the rugby side. John F. Peecock was also active in the local Conservative party and Henry was a member of the Junior Conservatives. Francis played for Ipswich between 1888 and 1892, travelling in from his home on the Finborough Road in Stowmarket. Like several of his schoolfellows and teammates, he became a solicitor and practised as part of the firm of Gudgeons, Peecock & Prentice.

C. L. Alexander (1874–1941)

Charles Leslie Alexander was born in Ipswich in December 1874, the son of William and Henrietta Alexander, and was part of the well-known Ipswich family of bankers. They lived at 27 Henley Road in Ipswich, near Christchurch Park. He was also a former pupil at Ipswich School and was 'Captain' of the school in 1891 (the equivalent of Head Boy). He also captained the school football and cricket teams. He went on to Shrewsbury public school and Trinity College Cambridge, where he was a football blue. He played cricket for Suffolk in 1909. He was a centre-forward for Ipswich Association Football Club between 1894 and 1899, scoring sixteen goals. He died in Islington, London in June 1941.

It is clear from these short biographical details that the players in the early days came from quite a narrow band of Ipswich society. There was already a strong connection between the families who owned local businesses and the club, and the circle around Ipswich School: wealthy, upper middle-class, privately educated, Conservative in politics, but with a benign, perhaps paternalistic, attitude to the people of Ipswich who made up their workforce. One such family, the Cobbolds, a well-established Ipswich family of brewers, politicians and dispensers of patronage to local writers and artists, played an almost dynastic role in the development of Ipswich Town Football Club that would eventually transform it beyond recognition to become one of the most exciting and successful English football teams of its day.

The Early Years

Early reports of Ipswich Association Football Club's matches do little to remove the impression that in those days it was more or less an Ipswich School football team. The following report from the *Ipswich Journal* on 23 November 1878 describes a typical match of that period:

> *Ipswich Association Football Club v. Woodbridge Grammar School.* This match was played on Saturday last, on the ground of the former, Broom Hill, Norwich Road, a large number of spectators being present, the result being an easy win for the home team by six goals to *nil* – G. S. Sherrington four, Burton two. W. S. Sherrington's corner kicking was much admired, and E. Turner's 'middling' was very effective.

In a series of articles written for the *Evening Star* in 1909, an Ipswich player, E. A. Kent, described what football was like in the town in the late nineteenth century. The first article is not about Ipswich Association Football Club specifically, but gives a vivid picture of what it was like to play the game then:

> I should much like to see a copy of the Rules of Football, as they stood in, say, 1880. They would not take long to get by heart, I imagine; they were so few as to be almost unnecessary, and much was left to the player's sense of honour. With practically no competition of any sort, games were what are now called 'friendlies', though the term would not always have applied exactly ... Players were assumed to be sportsmen at heart, who would, of course, keep in view the commandment 'Thou shalt not kill', but they were left the option of doing almost that, as far as the Rules were concerned...
>
> There was no imperial referee, no whistle; no ordering off the field. There were two umpires – one on each side of the ground – whose duty it was to keep the time, and to adjudicate in the matter of the scoring of goals, off-side, and the passing of the ball over the 'touch' lines ... These umpires were usually partisan, and most frequently disagreed, so that matches were reported ... as having resulted in, say, a tie of two goals each, with several others disputed. Very few clubs had cross-bars on their goalposts, but just a piece of tape or string, more or less taut, and it was sometimes difficult to tell if a high shot had gone under or over...
>
> They were fierce games that we played ... I have heard of men who had differences on the field that could be settled only in one way ... The game went on ten-a-side until (honour satisfied) the combatants returned to the fray with, perhaps, marks of the side issue visibly upon them.
>
> Our goalkeeper was Charlie Webb. Him it were unwise to provoke. He was surely the pioneer of the art of punching the ball far out of

danger; and he was perfectly willing to punch heads just as hard, and had frequently to be restrained from doing it.

In another article, Kent described a match he played for Ipswich Town at Portman Road in 1895, making it sound a little bit like something from the *Boy's Own Paper*:

In the hundreds of games that I played there have been many incidents that I shall never forget ... in the Amateur Cup, Ipswich Town *v.* Old Etonians, on the Portman Road ground – the fourth of that remarkable series of matches when the Ipswich Club was about at its zenith. I think it was one of the finest, keenest games I ever took a hand in; and played on a slippery ground on the first day of thaw after weeks of frost, it was very fast, indeed. Nevertheless, quite at the end I was in good condition enough to make the best of a very promising situation. The score was 1-1, and excitement fairly seethed. The ball came to me not far from the centre line, and I got fairly away from the half and well on the move for goal before the Old Etonians' defence scented danger. Hoare, the right-back, yelled to Heseltine, 'Look out, Christopher!' and the lanky Hampshire fast bowler came up with a raking stride to cut me off. It was difficult to turn at any time on slippery surface, and when speed was up, but one course was possible, and that a straight one, especially with the ball 'slithering' more than rolling. Alas, my direction was taking me to a point halfway between the goal-post and the corner flag, and the only chance at a shot seemed to be a long cue. That chance I took, and shot with as much force and as careful an aim as ever man set himself to accomplish. The ball went straight enough, but W. J. Seton was long and strong and alert, and he guided it over the bar. I have always been sure that what I did was best; but I sometimes still indulge in profitless hazards, and think of possible alternative dodges; but as they all partake of the acrobatic they may be dismissed as being not very feasible. I was told afterwards that I ought to have stopped with the ball, and the back would have gone by and left me a free course for goal!

Despite these glimpses into the past, it is very difficult to imagine what kind of people made up the growing body of Ipswich supporters at the time, but it's probably reasonable to speculate that some of them, at least, would have been the family and friends of the players and other people involved with the football club. As the kind of person who played for the club gradually changed over the years, so did the kind of people who came to support 'the Ipswich'.

The Road to the Football League

The two clubs, Ipswich Rugby Football Club and Ipswich Association Football Club, decided to amalgamate in September 1888. The move had been planned for some time and came about partly because the association club needed to move away from Brook's Hall, but also because interest in rugby in the town was declining. The ground at Portman Road had a more secure tenure and the pitch was in much better condition. It was decided that the football team would be called Ipswich Town Football Club and play in Oxford blue-and-white stripes. Blue and white had been the colours that the Ipswich School teams played in and they seem to have always been the Ipswich colours.

Ipswich Town did not become a professional football club until 1936, and joined the Football League two years later. The issue was debated, however, as early as April 1895, when the club was invited by Nat Whittaker to join the Southern League, which he had founded the previous year as a rival to the Football League because he believed that it was dominated by clubs from the Midlands and the North of England. A meeting was called on 9 April 1895 to consider whether Ipswich Town Football Club should join the Southern League. Several of the club's stalwarts spoke against it, including Francis Peecock who objected to the idea that football should become a business. It should be fun, he said, and added, to the hilarity of those present, 'Soon we shall be having Ipswich Town Ltd.'

George Sherrington had written to the *East Anglian Daily Times* before the meeting to warn against professionalism. The amateur ethic was still strong at Ipswich Town and would be for many years to come. Another argument made against joining the Southern League was the large amount of travelling that would result from joining a League involving teams as far away as Clapton Orient, Reading and Swindon Town.

At this stage of the proceedings, an amendment was moved by a local businessman, R. D. Hendry, that the club should join the Southern League and turn professional as well. However, no one at the meeting was even willing to second the amendment and it was therefore overwhelmingly defeated. It was very much a victory for the Ipswich School old boys. Ipswich Town Football Club would remain amateur and would not join the Football League for another four decades.

T. C. Cobbold died in 1883 and was replaced as president by a Holbrook-based magistrate, Benjamin Bridges Hunter Rodwell, a member of the Ipswich banking family. Educated at Charterhouse public school, he was a Conservative Member of Parliament between 1874 and 1881. The Cobbold family continued their connection with the club when the former president's brother, Nathanael Fromanteel Cobbold, was elected vice president at the club's Annual General Meeting in September 1885, although he died shortly afterwards.

The same season, 1885/86, saw the Churchmans, an Ipswich family whose small tobacconist's shop in Westgate Street would eventually grow to become a global brand, become involved both on and off the pitch. William Alfred Churchman played in goal (possibly only once) for Ipswich in the 1887/88 season and was on the club committee which had only five members. A staunch Conservative, who became Mayor of Ipswich in 1901, William would, with his brother Arthur Charles Churchman go on to transform his family firm into the tobacco giant, W. A. & A. C. Churchman. Their factory was adjacent to the Portman Road football ground and the south stand was known as Churchman's for many years.

In 1895, Captain Ernest Pretyman, of Orwell Park, became club president and was once again from the traditional background of Ipswich Town figureheads: a Conservative Member of Parliament, local landowner and a relation of the Cobbolds.

The new Portman Road-based Ipswich Town Football Club continued much as before, playing amateur matches against teams like Beccles, Long Melford and Framlingham College, either as friendlies or in the Suffolk Senior Cup. A change came at the beginning of the 1890/91 season, when it was announced that Town would not be entering the Senior Cup – which it had won for the past two seasons – but instead would take part in, what was then called the FA Challenge Cup for the first time.

Ipswich won the first of their matches in the qualifying round, against Reading at Portman Road, by two goals to nil. The team included some Town stalwarts: the Sherrington brothers, Stephen Notcutt, F. C. Peecock and E. A. Kent. Despite late pressure from the visiting side, Town were able to hold on to their early lead and go through to the next round, away against Norwich Thorpe.

A report on that match in the *East Anglian Daily Times* – which ended in a 4-0 victory for Ipswich – praised several Town players:

It would be almost invidious to select any of the visitors' forwards for praise, as they were all in excellent form. Sherrington and Kent seemed to create most impression amongst their opponents. The superiority of the Ipswich to the Norwich halves was a marked feature in the game.

Town almost went out of the tournament against Huntingdon County at Portman Road, partly due to a late train from Stowmarket, which meant they had to start the game without Francis Peecock, who commuted to matches from there by railway. After fifteen minutes' delay the referee decided that play should go ahead without him. Peecock eventually did get on to the field but it meant that Town made a poor start, although they eventually recovered. The *Ipswich Journal* reporter enthused:

A fast and well-contested game was witnessed at Ipswich on Saturday ... The Ipswich, although at the commencement of the game, apparently weak, soon showed that they had plenty of metal in them, and completely ran round their opponents in the latter half ... Peecock did not appear on the field until about ten minutes late ... When he did appear he was received with a cheer that seemed to put life in the Ipswich men.

Huntingdon took the lead twice in the first half, but Ipswich recovered to win 5-2, losing to the 93rd Highlanders in the final qualifying round and therefore not going through to the FA Cup proper. Nevertheless, it was an excellent debut in a tournament Town would go on to win eighty-seven years later.

By 1893, rugby had ceased to be played at Portman Road and Ipswich Town Football Club became an exclusively association football team, but still under the influence of the Old Ipswichian amateur ethic, the Committee refused to allow the first team to play in local leagues, and Ipswich Town continued to play a combination of friendly and cup matches. There was a growing feeling of resentment that Ipswich Town was falling behind other clubs because of this rather aloof approach. Other issues at this time included a growing demand for a proper stand to be built and the controversial subject of player transfers, which the amateurs who ran the club were opposed to. Matters came to a head at the club's Annual General Meeting on 30 August 1898, when what should have been a routine meeting turned rather stormy.

The meeting was attended by F. C. H. Gibbons, who had established the Suffolk and Ipswich Football League in 1896 after placing an advertisement in the *East Anglian Daily Times*. Announcing that he intended to launch a Football League for Ipswich and the surrounding area, he had arranged a meeting on 10 September 1896 which was attended by officials from eighteen clubs, including Ipswich Town, but when the League was formed, Ipswich Town was the only name missing.

When P. P. Cornell, the Ipswich Town club secretary, gave his annual report to the next Annual General Meeting, which concluded that performances on and off the pitch were satisfactory, it looked like it was business as usual, but F. C. H. Gibbons stood up, supposedly to second the report, and made remarks that were to cause a sensation. The following is based on newspaper reports of what was said at the meeting:

GIBBONS: The past season, under the existing conditions, might be fairly considered satisfactory, but I think I might say that those conditions are unsatisfactory. When I see this Town Club, supposed to be the representative club of the town, playing friendlies week after week, making no progress in other directions, I think I am justified in saying that it *is* unsatisfactory. The reason is due to the Committee who might be called 'slow coaches'. The Committee are totally insensible to the wants of the club. There is great friction concerning the composition of the teams, and also because the club is playing so many friendlies. Mr Cornell's idea of football, I believe, is very much like that of the fossilised amateur.

CORNELL: A genuine amateur.

GIBBONS: Mr Cornell doesn't believe in League matches or cup ties. The Committee have failed to progress with the times as other clubs have done. Our ground is one of the best in the Eastern Counties, but it is one of the worst appointed ... We need a complete reformation and, first of all, we need a good secretary – Mr Cornell cannot be described as an enterprising secretary. Everyone in the town who loves to the game wants to see different football, not friendlies week after week. We want a committee and a secretary who studies the interests of the Club *and* its supporters. The supporters are the mainstay of the Club: they provide the money. They don't want these friendlies. If we had a programme that included League matches – if the club entered, say, the Norfolk and Suffolk League – we would have bigger gates and more interest in the game. I believe we could double the 'gates' if we had better programmes. And when we've done that, the ground should be fitted up as it ought to be. We ought to have grandstands.

This, the county town, is far behind the times in this respect. If you go to North Suffolk you can find good stands, but at Ipswich there is only one and it's only good enough to use if it rains. It's not Mr Cornell's fault that Ipswich didn't enter the Norfolk and Suffolk League this season – that was due to the meeting being called so late. However, the fixtures that have been arranged can be cancelled.

CORNELL: Unsportsmanlike!

GIBBONS: I don't think that would be unsportsmanlike. We have the material in Ipswich to make this club the foremost in the county, instead of what it is – lagging behind all the others. We should also be bringing in good players from other clubs – I agree with the importation of players. Some of you may laugh, but I do not agree with you. [*Enthusiastic applause.*]

CORNELL: I hope you will tell us who these good players who are knocking about are. I think the Selection Committee knows football when it sees it. It's true that some men won't play in the [League] matches and I can understand why. The travelling involved takes up a good deal of time, more than most men can afford to give. We don't win all our matches, no club ever does. It's not our fault that the arrangement of the ground isn't better. The ground belongs to the Corporation, which leases it to certain gentlemen who are interested in sport and they let it at a nominal rental. There's been some talk of a bicycle track some day, and the football club having to go elsewhere. If we put up a stand, we might, in a year's time, have to go elsewhere and take the stand down. Our plans are more advanced than the average person knows of. If we scratch fixtures now, it will be the greatest act of unsportsmanship that we have ever known at this club – to scratch matches within two days of the opening of the season! London clubs look forward to playing us and some want to play us twice in a season. I regard competitive matches as undesirable and I think there is no more exemplary crowd in Suffolk than the Ipswich one. [*Applause.*] I'm sure that Mr Gibbons's criticisms are well meant and we take them as such. [*Cries of 'Hear, Hear!'*]

The effects of the meeting were not immediate, but it was evidence of how times were changing at Ipswich Town Football Club at the end of the nineteenth century. The old guard – players like the Sherringtons, Kent, the Peecocks and Cornell, the kernel of Ipswich School players who had been so important in the foundation of the club – were retiring, and with them the amateur ethic was disappearing too.

A look at the Ipswich Town Football Club side of the 1900/01 season shows how the background of the players was gradually changing. Although there were still some former Ipswich School boys, such as C. J. Palmer, Francis Cautley, Harry Steel and C. W. Alexander, and two clergymen, Revd M. J. Murray and Revd H. A. P. Gardiner played for the club, the rest of the side was made up of working-class men. Gerald Lewis, a clerk from Woodbridge who lived in a boarding house in Ipswich; Walter Cotton, who in 1901 was a carriage joiner, living in the poorest part of Ipswich, St Clement's parish; Scott Murdoch, a mechanical engineer living in Fore Street; and Albert Bailey, a painter and decorator. It may well be that these players were spotted when playing for some of the well-known works' teams in the town: Cowell's, Churchman's, Great Eastern Railway, Orwell Works and St Lawrence Works. Certainly Ernest Betts, a confectioner living in St Helen's parish, was brought in from the St Lawrence football team.

Ipswich Town did join the Norfolk and Suffolk League for the 1899/1900 season and finished fourth, but they were to remain an amateur club until 1936. Despite his misgivings, Philip Cornell eventually did come round to the idea that Ipswich Town should play in local Leagues and the club began the twentieth century by playing Beccles Caxton in the Norfolk and Suffolk League on 20 October 1900. Town won 8-0.

Ipswich Town's long-standing rivalry with Norwich City – which, of course, continues to this day – began in the 1902/03 season, when the Norfolk club was formed and joined the Norfolk and Suffolk League. League football was beginning to flourish in East Anglia and with the retirement of the old guard (E. A. Kent stopped playing for Town in 1903 and Philip Cornell, who had played as a goalkeeper since 1891, relinquished the captaincy to Vernon Lewis the same year and retired in 1906), Ipswich began to move away from its genteel, amateurish approach and, in fact, joined a second League competition in the 1903/04 season, the South East Anglian League.

In ten years, between 1895/96 and 1905/06, the first team went from playing only seven competitive matches (in two cup competitions) to playing thirty-two games a season, as well as continuing to play friendlies. At the same time, smaller clubs such as Ipswich Crown and St Clement Rangers were folding, and Town were able to recruit from a wider range of players. Two players from St Clement's who would be important for Ipswich Town in the years leading up to the First World War were the Double brothers, Ivan and William. Whether it was the impact of new blood or playing more competitive matches (although the captain, Lewis, complained they were playing too much), the 1903/04 season was a successful one. A 'huge' crowd gathered on Ipswich station on Saturday 19 March 1904 to greet the players who were bringing home two trophies: the Suffolk Senior Cup, which they had won that day by beating Leiston in front of 2,700 people at Hurt's Hall, Saxmundham, and the South East Anglian League trophy. Town would leave the South East Anglian League in 1906 following a dispute over unfulfilled fixtures.

Success on the pitch (Town won the Suffolk Senior Cup the following season too) brought pressure to develop Portman Road and with these plans came the necessity of forming a company. In November 1905, the fears of the club's gentlemen founders were realised when The Ipswich Cricket, Football and Athletic Ground Company Limited was formed. 2,000 shares were issued at a pound each. The first chairman was William Parker Burton of Burton Son & Saunders (and younger brother of Henry Bunnell Burton) and the vice chairman was Philip Wyndham Cobbold. A new lease was negotiated with the Corporation lasting for twenty-one years. Despite this commitment to development, the club was still influenced by its older members who wished to retain the amateur ethic.

George Sherrington in particular never changed his views on this matter and resigned his position as vice president of the Football Association to become involved with a new body, the Amateur Football Association, which in 1907 had split from the Football Association. The Norfolk and Suffolk League remained with the FA, but the Suffolk Football Association, undoubtedly under the influence of George Sherrington and Stephen Notcutt, defected to the Amateur Football Association. In future, Ipswich Town would play in the Southern Amateur League that was created in August 1907. This was in marked contrast to Norwich City, who became professional by default at the end of the 1904 season, only two years after the club's formation, having been deemed to be using professional methods, such as paying trainers and using a gymnasium, by a Football Association Commission of Inquiry.

Professional teams of largely working-class players were becoming dominant in football and it could be argued that figures like George Sherrington and Philip Cornell, no longer playing football but committee men determined to preserve what they had created, were holding Ipswich Town back.

By the time the First World War broke out in August 1914, Town had developed into an important local club, but they were heading downwards, towards mid-table mediocrity. During the 1912/13 season, a local newspaper columnist, 'Veteran', complained that some players were working all night on Fridays before playing on Saturday afternoon. In the three seasons running up to the outbreak of war, Town finished in the middle of the Southern Amateur League and were lagging behind rivals like the New Crusaders, the Civil Service and the Casuals, only just finishing above the Crouch End Vampires in the 1913/14 season on goal difference. From being part of the club's founding values, amateurism was now becoming a problem for Ipswich Town.

3

War

The First World War

One Ipswich Town player lost his life during the Boer Wars, but neither the club nor the town had been as affected by a military conflict as they were to be by the First World War. At the outbreak of war, in August 1914, it was a popularly held belief that the conflict would be over quickly, even 'by Christmas'.

Professional football – which did not involve Ipswich Town, who were playing in the Southern Amateur League at that time – continued. The organisations that controlled the game, the Football League and the Southern League, announced that their players were on legally binding contracts and fixtures would therefore carry on as usual. The clubs attempted to do their part by allowing the military to use their grounds for drill. Crowds listened to patriotic speeches before matches, men were urged to enlist and collections were taken for war relief funds.

At first this went down well with the public and the national press. On the first day of the 1914/15 season, *The Times* reported that:

> After a meeting of the Consultative Committee of the Football Association in London yesterday, it was stated that the War Office opinion was favourable to the continuance of football ... Mr J. C. Clegg, who presided, appealed to every man who was capable of rendering personal service to his country to do so at once. He believed the suspension of all games would be mischievous, and that football players and spectators were as prepared to do their duty as any other section of the community. He urged clubs to give all possible assistance by releasing players during the war.
>
> The Football League has recommended each club to arrange for their players to undergo special military drill and for the provision of the miniature rifle range to provide ample shooting practice.

But as the war got off to a disastrous start for the British Expeditionary Force and the death toll rose, the press soon identified professional footballers as the villains of the piece. *The Times* reported on recruitment at football matches on 24 November 1914:

> At the recruiting centres yesterday there was a feeling of disappointment at the failure of the recruiting meetings at the football grounds on Saturday. In some quarters it is held that the mere continuance of the professional game is in itself a deterrent to the young men who watch matches. 'It has a moral effect,' said one recruiting officer. 'These professional footballers of England are the pick of the country for fitness. Nobody has a right to say that any body of men are not doing their duty ... but when the young men week after week see the finest physical manhood of the country expending its efforts in kicking a ball about, they can't possibly realise that there is a call for every fit man at the front.

On the letters page of the same edition of *The Times*, this typical example from 'An Old Player' was published:

> Sir – The statistics published in *The Times* of to-day of the attendances at football matches and the resultant recruiting are disheartening.
>
> Who is to blame? Is it the professional footballer, who, by playing, diverts the minds of the manhood of this country from the sterner things across the Channel, or is it the director of the football club registered as a limited liability company? It cannot be denied that certain clubs are run as much for profit as any other business organisation. If the clubs were run for the game only the present high rate of wages would not be paid to retain the most skilful players. If as much patriotism exists among followers of professional footballers as they would like us to believe, why have not the employers followed the commendable lead of big Rugby clubs and closed down altogether while serious business confronts the nation?

Another letter, by Walter N. Landor, suggested that if the football clubs would not act, Parliament should pass a law to make the taking of gate receipts for football matches illegal and suggested that a 'special regiment of professional footballers could be formed'.

Eventually, regimental teams were set up and the *East Anglian Daily Times* regularly featured team photographs as well as reporting stories of atrocities committed by the 'barbarous Germans'. Weekly lists of the names of young men who enlisted were also a regular item in the local press. The Old Ipswichians were actively involved in the recruitment campaign.

Tragically, the Ipswich area was affected very early on in the war when on 25 August 1914 the 2nd Battalion Suffolk Regiment, part of the 14th Brigade of the BEF, came under attack at Le Cateau as they were retreating from the Battle of Mons. Reports of casualties vary. It is believed that 720 Suffolks were lost, either killed, missing or wounded. It is believed that more than 500 men were taken as prisoners of war.

Even though Ipswich Town was not then a professional club, and therefore not involved in the national outcry against footballers, the pressure upon local players, as fit young men in 'the best physical condition', to join up would have been very strong. Footballers may have been regarded as being among the fittest, but the general population of Ipswich would probably not have been in very good physical condition at that time. Poverty and malnutrition were widespread. In 1913, the *Evening Star* had organised a competition for the 'wives of labourers' in Ipswich earning less than £1 a week. The wife who could write the best description of how to bring a family up on 'a quid a week', would win a sovereign.

The growing number of working-class Ipswich Town players who had been recruited from works teams like Cowell's or Orwell Works would probably have not been well nourished, but they would have been more physically fit, perhaps, than average and under tremendous social pressure to fight for their country, and join up they did.

None of the men who played for Ipswich Town in the immediate period before the First World War returned to play for the team afterwards. This was partly because of age, because Portman Road was requisitioned by the War Office and would not return the ground to the club until 1920, Town would not play again as a football team for six years and many of the pre-war players would have been too old to play at that level again. Portman Road was used firstly for training recruits and later for storing heavy military equipment, which left the pitch in such a bad state that it took a great deal of time and effort to restore it to a playable condition.

Little is known about the wartime experiences of most of the Ipswich Town footballers who played in the period immediately before the First World War, but three of them – Allan Bowman, Cecil Fenn and Claude Sennitt – were killed and Ernie Bugg, who was one of Town's leading goalscorers, lost his leg.

Ernest Arthur Bugg was an inside-forward who made his debut for Ipswich against Ealing in October 1911. Signed from Westbourne Mills, Ernie scored a total of seventy-nine goals in sixty-two appearances. He was a plumber by trade, the son of a painter and decorator, who is recorded in the 1911 Census as living with his parents at No. 155 Bramford Road, Ipswich. It's not known in what circumstances he lost his leg – apart from that he was fighting in France – but it obviously put an end to his life as a talented amateur footballer. He died in Ipswich in 1946. The H. Bugg who played one game for Ipswich against The Casuals in the Southern Amateur League in November 1911 may well have been Ernie's older brother, Harry.

Cecil Frank Fenn was born at Gould House in Dedham, Essex on 25 March 1890. Along with his brother, Charles, he was a regular and highly regarded player for Ipswich Town, making a total of sixty-six appearances and scoring nineteen goals between 1908 and 1913. When not playing football, he worked in Ipswich as a brewer's clerk, probably for the family firm, as his father, Cooper Fenn, was described in the 1891 census as a brewer as well as a 'political registrar and agent'. Charles Deane Fenn, brother of Cecil, played for Ipswich for five seasons between 1905 and 1912. He was a talented sportsman, who played in the Southern Amateur League XI on several occasions. Both brothers decided to emigrate, Charles to India and Cecil to British Columbia.

Charles Fenn returned from India many years later and died in Ipswich, aged eighty-five, in 1974. Cecil's fate was rather different. He was such a popular football player that when he left Ipswich a crowd accompanied him to the railway station to cheer him off. His plan had been to be a fruit farmer in Canada, but the First World War intervened. He enlisted in Princess Patricia's Canadian Light Infantry and returned to Europe as a soldier. Private Fenn was killed in action during the Second Battle of Ypres at Bellewaerde Lake in Belgium on 4 May 1915, aged twenty-five. He was buried at Menin Gate Memorial.

Claude Cushing Sennitt played for Town between 1909 and 1912. He was born in Norwich on 7 February 1892 and played as an inside-forward, making twenty-four appearances and scoring eleven goals. Sub-Lieutenant Sennitt was the eldest son of Mr and Mrs Sennitt of Brundall in Norfolk. At the age of nineteen, while he was playing for Ipswich Town, he was lodging in a boarding house in Aspley Road, Great Yarmouth and working as a 'provision merchant's clerk'. He joined the Royal Naval Volunteer reserve, Hood Battalion in 1916, and left for the front at the beginning of April 1917. He died from a gunshot wound to his right thigh on 23 April the same year.

Allan T. Bowman was a centre-half for Ipswich Town between 1907 and 1911. He was probably a tailor's son from St Helen's parish who was born in 1885. Little is known about him, but he appears as a casualty on the Suffolk Roll of Honour as a Lance Corporal in the Royal Fusiliers. His medal record card in the National Archives has a note written in September 1918 which 'requests permission for disposal of medals'.

Frederick Thomas Ellis was born on 19 August 1894, the son of a printer's compositor and grew up in Chevallier Street, Ipswich. He worked as a pattern maker for the engineering firm, Reavell & Co., on Ranelagh Road. The company, which later became Compair Reavell and employed many Ipswich people over the years, closed down in October 2012. Fred was a centre-forward who made his Town debut against the Crouch End Vampires in the Southern Amateur League in November 1913. He scored five goals in the League that season, plus six in the Amateur Football Association Cup, including four in one game in the second round. In old age, he recalled in an interview with the authors of *The Men Who Made The Town* that he wrote to the Ipswich Town secretary, Frank Mills, asking for a ball so that he and his comrades could play football at the front. He joined up early on, on 4 September 1914; despite this, he survived the war and died in 1990 at the age of ninety-six. He did not return to playing football after the First World War, even though he was only twenty-six when matches resumed at Portman Road and the 1913/14 season remained the only one in which he played.

Russell Johnson Hemnell, was another Norfolk-based player. Born in Norwich on 16 April 1890, he had played for Norwich Teachers, Norwich CEYMS, Norwich City, St John's Battersea and Croydon Common, before joining Town in October 1913. He played at outside-right, made seventeen appearances and scored six goals before he left in April 1914. He joined the sixth Norfolk Regiment and served as a Corporal in France, where he met the woman who was to become his wife, Jeanne Amélie Du Laurens. In later life he was a teacher and headmaster and served the Norfolk County FA for fifty-two years, including as its chairman and president.

Although Zeppelins dropped bombs on East Anglian towns and villages, the civilian population was not affected as badly as it would be during the Second World War. Yet following the enormous loss of life on the killing fields of France and Belgium, the country was left in a state of massive national bereavement. The total number of British soldiers, sailors and airmen killed in action, including those who died of wounds, disease or injury, or who were missing, presumed dead was 956,703. An influenza epidemic that swept around the world in 1919 added almost a quarter of a million to the death toll, among a population already weakened and depressed by four years of war. In her brilliant evocation of that period, *Testament of Youth*, Vera Brittain described what it felt like to be young in the immediate aftermath of war:

An exhausted world as divine normality, the spring of life after the winter of death, the stepping-stone to a new era, the gateway to an infinite future – a future not without its dreads and discomforts, but one in whose promise we had to believe, since it was all that some of those had left to believe in.

Those young people who were left turned to hedonism and fun as a release from the suffering of the war years. Sport – particularly football – became extremely popular, as Robert Graves and Alan Hodge, the authors of a social history of that period, *The Long Weekend*, described:

> Between the Football Association, which controlled professional football, and the Amateur Football Association, which had broken away from it many years before the war, there was a polite truce. The well-to-do classes had a strong prejudice against professional Association football as mercenary, venial and unsporting, and the Select Press published only the briefest reports on even First Division League matches with gates of hundreds of thousands. This was old-fashioned, for FA football was now at least as clean as the amateur variety – the crowds execrated any dirty play, the integrity of referees was beyond suspicion, and hard training had raised the level of professional skill to a point where even the best amateur team could not seriously compete. Every year the Corinthians, a club drawn from public-school football, entered for the Football Cup; but their kick and rush tactics and shoulder-charges, though disconcerting, never succeeded against the close passing and well-drilled manouevres of the professional teams which they met. The amateur's chief scorn was for the end of season sale of players.

Becoming a Professional Club

After long, drawn-out negotiations with Ipswich Town Football Club, the War Office eventually returned Portman Road and even agreed to pay some compensation. The ground staff, under Stephen Notcutt, worked hard to return the pitch to a playable state, but the club had to make a public appeal for new players for the 1920/21 season. The new players included a soldier stationed locally, Lionel ('Len') Mizen. Born in West Ham in 1895, Len had lived in Walthamstow and worked as a printer for the Bank of England before the war. He was a centre-forward for Town and scored forty-six goals in fifty-three matches. His greatest moment may have been when he scored a winning goal at Portman Road in a friendly against Chelsea in May 1921, a game that featured two international players for the visiting side. Mizen's health was poor – this may have been a result of the war or the influenza pandemic – and it affected his career badly. He died in Ipswich in 1929 at the age of thirty-three.

Chelsea, a professional club in the First Division of the Football League, tried to sign another Ipswich player, Bert Haste, who also received the offer of a professional contract from Hull City. Although the offer must have been tempting to Haste, who worked at the Churchman's tobacco factory while he played for Town, he had another vocation and turned both offers down on the advice of his father. He would later become a clergyman, spending many years in India as a missionary. His brother, Beauford, also played football for the club and became a minister nearer to home at Felixstowe.

Ipswich Town won the Southern Amateur League title in 1922 and about 4,000 supporters formed a victory parade, in which the players were transported from the railway station to the Cornhill by lorry to celebrate. A consequence of the war years, however, was that there was still some resentment about the 'unpatriotic' continuation of association football during the conflict, and both Ipswich School and Framlingham College decided to adopt rugby as their official sport, further loosening the connections between the old guard and the club.

Town's fortunes at that time were affected by many external factors, including players turning professional and moving to other clubs, and the fact that several players, such as W. W. Dempsey and Len Mizen, remained in the armed forces and would sometimes be obliged to play for service teams instead of their regular clubs. Dempsey would eventually turn professional and play for Norwich City. Other servicemen who played regularly for Town included Corporal L. Taylor (centre-forward 1925/26), Airman J. Lister (who played only four times in the 1925/26 season), L. F. Smith (1925–35), all based at RAF Martlesham, and Petty Officer J. Marshall, who made twelve appearances between 1926 and 1928 and was from HMS *Ganges*.

Another serviceman was Flight-Lieutenant S. N. Webster, who was based at RAF Martlesham. He played sixty-nine matches for Ipswich Town, became club captain and was described as an 'extremely competitive' player. Sidney Webster was born in Walsall in 1900 and joined the Royal Air Force in 1918. Webster played at left back for Town between 1925 and 1930, but he became internationally famous when he won the Coupe d'Aviation Maritime Jacques Schneider (better known as the Schneider Trophy) a speed competition for seaplanes. Sponsored by a financier, balloonist and aircraft enthusiast of that name, the race was held eleven times between 1913 and 1931. Webster won a race held in Venice in 1927 when he flew a Supermarine S5 single-engined seaplane at an average speed of 281.66 mph (453 km/h). He had an immensely successful career in aviation and became an Air Vice-Marshal in the RAF, retiring in 1950.

The 1920s saw the death of three of the most influential figures from the club's early days: Philip Cornell, Francis Peecock and Stephen Notcutt, again removing some of the ties with the Old Ipswichians and the culture of amateurism. At the same time, ambition at Portman Road was growing. At the end of the 1926/27 season, Town appointed its first professional trainer, Edwin Dutton, a former Newcastle United player. Dutton is widely regarded as being extremely influential in transforming Ipswich into a much more competitive and successful football team which would mean that, a decade later, it would be fully prepared for professional and Football League status. It would also be the beginning of a continuing connection between the club and the North East of England up to and beyond the arrival of Bobby Robson in 1969.

Born in 1890, probably in Newcastle upon Tyne but possibly in Germany, Edwin Dutton was certainly living in Berlin with his parents from a young age as his father ran a sports shop there. Edwin played at outside-right for two Berlin clubs and in one international match for Germany against Hungary in 1909. He returned to England in 1910 to play as an amateur for Newcastle United and married the daughter of the famous Newcastle trainer, James McPherson. Dutton was in Germany at the outbreak of the First World War and, despite the fact that he had represented that country at football, was interned because of his English background. After managing the Stuttgart Kickers, he became a trainer for South Shields before arriving at Ipswich in 1927, where he was the closest thing to a manager that Town had employed up to that date. He left the club to return to the North East in 1932 and was given a rousing send-off and a gift of 'a handsome rosewood clock'.

Although Dutton was briefly replaced as trainer by Herbert Dainty, who had worked at Nottingham Forest and Leicester City among other clubs, he maintained a connection with Ipswich when his nephew, Bob McPherson, who been working in the Netherlands with Dutch club HDS, took on the role in 1934.

In February 1935, Ipswich Town and eleven other clubs founded the Eastern Counties League, and four months later one of the most influential figures in the club's history became president: John Murray Cobbold, a former Army Captain, who was always known by his nickname, Ivan. He had been president of the Suffolk Football Assoiation for two years, and would be the man who would turn Ipswich Town professional and take them into the Football League.

Although the new Eastern Counties League was amateur, moves for the club to turn professional were gathering momentum. Leonard Thompson, a young builder's clerk, led a letter-writing campaign to the local press seeking the foundation of a professional football club, Ipswich United, based at either Portman Road, the Suffolk Greyhound Stadium or a newly built stadium and even going so far as to register the club's new colours: red-and-white stripes. Among the men who wanted to be on the new club's board of directors were Robert Cobbold, Alderman R. F. Jackson and Nat Shaw, who also happened to be the owner of the greyhound stadium.

It is almost certain that there were vested business interests involved in the setting up of the new company. Thompson worked for Parkington & Sons, who had built the Hippodrome and were interested in the potential of developing the Greyhound Stadium as a replacement for Portman Road, so the presence of figures closely associated with it suggests an interest wider than that of involvement with the football club. The plan was to increase the greyhound stadium's capacity to 30,000, and £5,000 had already been pledged by those who wanted the plan to go ahead. However, the first meeting in April 1936 rejected the proposal and voted that Ipswich Town Football Club would remain amateur, although it remained a possibility that the new professional outfit, Ipswich United, might use Portman Road for matches alternating with the amateur Ipswich Town side. The situation changed rapidly when Ivan Cobbold – who had been in Canada – was approached by Ipswich United and wrote a letter to the *Evening Star* enthusing about the idea of professional football at Ipswich Town. His backing was the crucial piece of the jigsaw that would make it possible for those who wanted professional status to achieve their aims. His connections with senior figures in the football world, such as Suffolk-born Stanley Rous, secretary of the Football Association and Arsenal chairman, Samuel Hill-Wood, must have been helpful. Less than a month later, on 1 May 1936, in a meeting at the Town Hall, the following resolution was passed:

> That the Ipswich Town Football Club amalgamate with the proposed Ipswich United Football Club Ltd, and Ipswich Town Football Club Ltd be formed to run a professional team in the Southern League and an amateur team in the Eastern Counties League at Portman Road, Ipswich, and a combined committee to be formed without delay with a view to working out the necessary details; and that the consent of the Ipswich Corporation and the Ground Syndicate be obtained as soon as possible.

Leonard Thompson became club secretary and also chairman of the recently formed Supporters' Association. The board of the new company had both familiar and new names: local aristocracy Lord Cranworth, Douglas Tollemache and Sir Charles Bunbury, as well as Conservative party supporting businessmen, Ivan and Robert Cobbold, Harold Hooper, Nat Shaw and Robert Jackson, and the Unionist MP for Ipswich, Sir John Ganzoni. Sir Samuel Hill-Wood, who was chairman of Arsenal Football Club, became vice president and Ivan Cobbold's frequent visits to the north London stadium were influential in creating the vision that the latter had for Ipswich Town Football Club. The professional club's first manager, Mick O'Brien, was interviewed for the job at Highbury.

Michael O'Brien (1893–1940) was assistant manager at Brentford following a spell managing Queens Park Rangers. He had played football for many clubs, including Glasgow Celtic, Brooklyn Wanderers and Norwich City, and had also won international caps for Ireland. Town decided that they would not pay transfer fees until they were elected to the Football League, but that didn't stop O'Brien from bringing in players such as George Perrett from Fulham, Freddy Houldsworth from Stoke City, former Hearts and Barrow player Charlie Cowie and, most impressively of all, Jimmy McLuckie, from Aston Villa – despite the fact that the twenty-eight-year-old half-back had been transfer listed for £2,000.

It seems there was national goodwill for Ipswich Town Football Club from the beginning of its professional era. The *Daily Sketch* of 29 August 1936 featured the club on its back page, which was decorated with caricatures of the manager and the players: Jackie Williams, Bobby Bruce, Jock Carter, Jack Blackwell, George Dobson, Fred Houldsworth, Oswald Parry, Bob Thomson, George Perrett, Charles Cowie, Jimmy McLuckie and trainer Bob McPherson. Under the headline 'The Right Switch By Ipswich', L. V. Manning wrote:

> Ipswich's quick switch ... from an amateur to professional football was never a gamble. It was backing a certainty.
>
> The bold adventurers who have raised the flag of professionalism in this stronghold of exclusive FA football are no visionaries. They will find their justification at the turnstiles this afternoon when the curtain goes up on a season which makes history in the old Suffolk town.
>
> Before the first click is registered by the first spectator – who, I wonder, will get up early enough to win this distinction? I am going to make two prophecies.
>
> The first is that Ipswich Town will be a Football League club within two seasons, and the second is that before two months of the season is past the big League buyers will be buzzing around Mick O'Brien making bids for Jimmy McLuckie and Bobbie Bruce.
>
> Some of them haven't waited for the season to start! Would the Town let these or any of their young stars go if the cheques were of tempting proportions?
>
> I believe in asking direct questions. So ... I put this bluntly to my old friend the O'Brien: 'The best answer I can give you is to quote the chairman, Captain Cobbold,' he replied. 'We are builders, not sellers.'
>
> 'You can take it as official that no offers will be even considered,' went on the Town manager. 'We have set out to bring class League football to Ipswich, and I believe we have the team to do it. However glittering the offers, my directors fully realise the folly of breaking up a side. Small clubs can't rise that way.'

So from the very start a pattern was set, and it would be many years until Ipswich Town abandoned this policy of building its squad up gradually and not being a 'selling club'. It would be a policy that stood the club in very good stead.

Over the years, Ipswich Town earned a reputation for not sacking its managers either, but this was not the case with their first. Despite success on the pitch – winning the Southern League, qualifying for the FA Cup proper, only to go out in the second round and beating Norwich City in the Hospital Cup at Portman Road – and what has been described as a 'happy atmosphere' at the club, and despite all the indications predicting that his second season at Ipswich Town would be even more successful, O'Brien was summarily sacked. Ivan Cobbold released a terse statement that betrayed a certain ruthlessness that has rarely been associated with the Cobbold family, but appears to have risen to the surface from time to time:

O'Brien is no longer anything whatever to do with Ipswich Town FC. I suppose in due course a new secretary-manager will be appointed but the Board will be in no hurry. I am confident we can carry on for the time being. The players are absolutely happy and this is not going to upset them at all.

The club remained silent about the reasons for O'Brien's suspension and various explanations have been speculated upon, including an extra-marital affair. We know that O'Brien's wife had died shortly after he was appointed as manager, but it is very difficult to discover very much personal information about him. One of his obituaries in the *Derby Daily Telegraph* on 26 September 1940 (he had been a player at Derby County between 1926 and 1928) reveals a little about his character: 'He was a stickler for his rights, and I can recall a futile effort to make him talk in the desired strain in a hotel in Birmingham at the time of his linking up with the "Rams".'

It seems unlikely that the suspension of a successful manager so soon after being offered a new contract was for some kind of moral issue. The Cobbolds were not known to be deeply puritanical. Newspapers reports referred to O'Brien as being instantly 'suspended from taking further part in the activities of the club' following a board meeting in August 1937. This swift and rather brutal action on the part of Ivan Cobbold suggests some kind of serious misconduct, but it is unlikely that the truth will ever emerge unless some relevant personal correspondence is discovered.

O'Brien had taken on club secretary's duties when Leonard Thompson became ill at the start of the 1936/37 season, and the role of secretary-manager would continue for many years, the manager being responsible for everything at the club, from general administration to contract negotiations, as well as coaching. Thompson's illness ended his formal association with the club, but he was to be made its first life member in recognition of his services to the club, particularly in bringing it up to professional level.

Adam Scott Mattheson Duncan (1888–1976), O'Brien's successor, was very much in the secretary-manager mould having served in that role for Hamilton Academical, Cowdenbeath and, from 1932 to 1937 for Manchester United. He was famously almost abducted from Manchester United – or so, at least, the story goes – when Ivan Cobbold sent a car to collect Duncan, leaving a case of vintage port behind in 'payment'. Behind the legend lies some ruthless ambition on the part of the Ipswich board. One of the reasons that Scott Duncan was brought to the club was that he had a great many contacts in the football world, and was able to command the votes when it came to the final decision about whether or not Ipswich Town should replace Gillingham in the Football League. Duncan was to receive a salary of £2,000 *per annum*, with a bonus of £1,000 if the club entered the Football League and promises of further similar sums if he could take Ipswich up to the very top. It is clear that the club now had serious plans to become one of the biggest clubs in England. Ossie Parry, who was Ipswich Town's first professional footballer, told the *Evening Star* in an interview in 1988, when he was aged seventy-nine, 'There was a lot of ambition about Ipswich. They may have been non-League at the time but they clearly wanted to go places.'

Always dressed immaculately, in a dark suit and his trademark homburg hat, Scott Duncan resembled a bank manager more than a football coach, and indeed his role was very much that of an administrator. His salary was large for the time, but he was a tough negotiator when it came to the players' contracts. Players were happy to come to Ipswich Town in this era, though, and Duncan made some impressive signings, including Mick Burns, the Preston goalkeeper. The consequent improvement began to make an immediate impact on the team's success on the football field even before the club joined the Football League.

The meeting at which Town were admitted to the League took place on 30 May 1938 in London. The Ipswich Town Football Club deputation comprised of Ivan and Robert Cobbold, Nat Shaw, Herbert Foster, along with the manager and his assistant, Scott Duncan and Don Read. The fate of Walsall and Gillingham was also being considered that day. The vote in the end was Ipswich Town thirty-six, Walsall thirty-four and Gillingham twenty-eight. Ipswich Town Football Club was now a member of the Football League and would never look back. Town's success was reported across the country. On 31 May 1938, the *Western Daily Press* reported the 'Sensational Defeat of Gillingham' thus:

In a quiet, wavering voice, Mr C. E. Sutcliffe, announced to the representatives of the Football League clubs at the annual meeting in London yesterday that Ipswich Town had been elected and that Gillingham had lost their place in the Southern Section of the Third Division.

The defeat of Gillingham was regarded as sensational, because a few weeks before the southern section clubs had recommended Gillingham for re-election, and Town had come a poor third behind Walsall in the vote. It's not possible to discover exactly what changed things so dramatically, although Ipswich had campaigned hard, spending a large amount of money on lobbying officials and producing an expensive glossy brochure about the club and the town. One main selling point was that Town's growing support meant their average 'gate' in 1937/38 was over 9,000, which compared favourably with many Third Division clubs in the south of England. Town's ambitions were to be temporarily thwarted, however, and they would only play one full season in the Third Division (South) before the Second World War. It was a successful first season, and the club finished seventh in the League, including some notable victories over Somerset side, Street (7-0), Watford (5-1) and Aldershot (7-2). Football League status allowed Ipswich Town Football Club to attract players from well-established clubs, like Fred Chadwick, who signed from Newport County but who had previously played for Wolves and scored four of the goals in the heavy defeat of Street.

The Second World War

The Second World War, which was declared in September 1939, had an even greater impact on the civilian population of Ipswich than the First World War. Ipswich was one of a number of British towns targeted by the German Luftwaffe for 'Coventration': concentrated bombing aimed at massive destruction and the resulting demoralisation of the people there. The term was coined following the destruction of the centre of the Midland city of Coventry by a German *Blitzkrieg*. Ipswich was bombed over fifty times between June 1940 and March 1945. Fifty-three people were killed and a considerable number more were injured or lost their homes. Ipswich was the target of the Luftwaffe because of its docks and railway links, as well as being an important centre of the engineering industry, but bombs fell across the entire town – it was not uncommon for pilots to empty their remaining load randomly on the East Anglian coast. In one raid, near Nacton Road, a woman and her eight children were killed.

The football ground at Portman Road, despite being close to the railway and not far from the docks and Ipswich's industrial area, was not directly hit, although an RAF bomber, according to eye-witnesses, crashed into the river Orwell after attempting to land on the pitch when one of its engines failed.

Town had played only three matches in the 1939/40 season before war was declared. On 3 September 1939, the club staff listened to the Prime Minister, Neville Chamberlain, announce to the nation over the 'wireless' that war had been declared on Germany. Former Town player Jackie Little recalled in an interview with Mel Henderson, published in the *Evening Star* in 1993, 'There were thirty-five players, plus the office boy, sitting in the dressing room listening to the radio. When the announcement came over, our insurance cards were stamped and we were sacked on the spot.'

Ivan Cobbold, once again showing a ruthless determination where Ipswich Town was concerned, made what appears to be a unilateral decision to end professional football for the duration of the war, although it was reported in the press as the decision of the board of directors. *The Times* report on the 14 September 1939 indicates just how quick off the mark the club was:

> The Lancashire Football Association at their meeting in Preston yesterday permitted a resumption of football in specified areas in Lancashire subject to the consent of the police, but barred competitive games for the present.
>
> The Ipswich Town Football Club directors yesterday decided unanimously that football at Ipswich shall be suspended indefinitely. Ipswich is not a banned area.

Other clubs, including Colchester United and Norwich City, continued to play during the war – sometimes at Portman Road – and some players, such as Ossie Parry, Mick Burns, Jimmy McLuckie, Jackie Little and Fred Chadwick, made guest appearances for the Canaries while serving in the armed forces.

Jackie Little became a Physical Training Instructor (PTI) with the rank of sergeant in the RAF. Born in Blaydon, near Gateshead, in 1912, John Little was the son of a coalminer and one of ten children. He was a surface worker at a pit until he was eighteen, but his father wanted a different life for him. 'My old man wouldn't hear of it,' he told the *Evening Star* in an interview in 1993. 'Nearly everyone that came out of the pits ended up a cripple and he didn't want any more of his kids down there.' Failing to find any alternative employment in his native North East, Little moved to Suffolk where he trained as a carpenter. He also became a footballer, playing at first for Needham Market. After two years he went for a trial with Ipswich Town and signed amateur terms in 1936, making his debut against local rivals Stowmarket Town in the first round of the FA Cup when he scored one of the goals (Ipswich won 8-0). He continued to earn his living in a variety of ways, working as a carpenter, an egg delivery man, and a fitter's mate at £2 a week, until he turned professional in November

1937, shortly before new manager Scott Duncan arrived. Little played as a forward, making 200 appearances for Town before and after the war. During the war, he was stationed near Bath and played for Bath City, sometimes playing alongside Stan Mortensen of Blackpool and England.

True to their paternalistic style, the Cobbolds arranged for some of the players to work either in their own brewery or for local firms: the manager, Scott Duncan, was found work with Churchman's tobacco factory although he was also paid a weekly 'retainer' by Ivan Cobbold.

Ossie Parry was the club's first professional footballer – he was signed by Mick O'Brien from Crystal Palace in 1936 and subsequently served six years in the RAF as a Leading Aircraftman (LAC). He was a full-back and one of many players whose careers were shortened by war, but he was already thirty years old when war broke out – the club had 'misinformed' the press about his age when he had signed – but he returned in 1945, only to retire in 1950 at the age of forty-two when he went to work for the Cobbolds' brewery.

Fred Chadwick was a prolific centre-forward, who had made his name as an amateur player for the Manchester-based team, British Dyes. He signed for Ipswich in June 1938 and so, regrettably, spent a very short time at the club. Between signing and the cessation of football at Portman Road, he made forty-one appearances and scored twenty-three goals, seventeen in Division Three. In the early years of the war he made guest appearances for Norwich City (he scored four times for the Canaries against Aldershot in 1940), Bolton Wanderers, Clapton Orient and Oldham Athletic, but he later joined the Army, was captured by the Japanese in Singapore and was sent to work as a slave labourer on the Burma-Siam railway. It has often been written that he did not play football again following his wartime experiences, but in fact he returned to play for Town in the 1946/47 season, playing six times in the League and scoring once. He signed for Bristol Rovers in 1947 and for the Somerset side, Street, in 1948 but retired from professional football in May 1949 at the age of thirty-five, which was not particularly early for a player at that time. His daughter, Sally Hawkins, wrote on the Pride of Anglia website:

> This was my dad. He was born 08.11.1913 and died 18.09.1987. He had five children and was married to Nancy for nearly fifty years. He lived and breathed football right to the end.

Mick Burns made 171 appearances for Ipswich as a goalkeeper before and after the Second World War, and played in Town's first-ever Football League game on 27 August, 1938. Born in Leeholme, near Bishops Auckland, he was one of several players who came to Town from the

North East, possibly exploiting the connections built up by trainers Dutton and McPherson. He played for Newcastle United between 1927 and 1936, then went to Preston North End, where he played in the 1937 FA Cup final, but signed for Ipswich as he thought they were an 'up and coming club'. He was a Lance-bombardier in the Army during the war, serving in Italy and North Africa, but returned to play for Ipswich. Described by those who knew him as 'a real Gent' and 'a brilliant man', he played for Town until he was forty-three years old, only retiring in October 1951.

Charles Cowie, who had come to Ipswich from Barrow in 1936, would have a long and important relationship with the club. Known as Charlie, he played for Town fifty-two times before the war. He joined the Army in 1939 and was a guest player for King's Park, near Stirling, in his native Scotland. After returning to Suffolk, he became the reserve trainer at Ipswich Town from 1945–65, but is also remembered, with his wife Christina, for looking after many young players in his own home during that time.

Billy Dale had played for both Manchester United and Manchester City (where he was part of the 1934 FA Cup-winning side) before he signed for Ipswich in 1938. He made forty-four appearances for Town as a full-back. Born in 1905, he joined the Army during the war, which effectively ended his footballing career, as he was over forty years old by the time it ended. He made a guest appearance for Norwich City during the war, but worked as a plumber afterwards. He died in his native Manchester in 1987.

Bryn Davis (his full name was Albert Brynley Davies) had already been in the Army before he signed for Cardiff City in 1935 and so was one of the first players to join up when war broke out. He joined Ipswich Town in 1938, playing as an inside-forward and was described in one newspaper report as 'simply mesmerising'. He made thirty-nine appearances and scored nine goals. Injuries received in battle meant that he was unable to play football after 1945, and he became a scout for Bristol City and Cardiff City. He died in 1990, aged seventy-six.

George Perrett also played for Ipswich Town as a half-back before and after the Second World War. He signed from Fulham in 1936 and was another member of the team that played in Town's first League match against Southend United. He served in the Army during the war and was involved in the D-Day landing in Normandy in 1944. He returned to play regularly for Town after the war, retiring in June 1950 having made a total of 206 appearances.

Jimmy McLuckie, Town's star signing from Aston Villa and the club's first professional captain, joined the Home Guard. He was thirty-one when war broke out, although he looked considerably older. McLuckie played as a guest for various clubs throughout the war and also for the Home Guard. The *Essex Chronicle* reported on one such match on 30 October 1942:

A strong Home Guard team, captained by Pte. Jimmy McLuckie, defeated a Royal Navy XI, from Chatham 4-1 on the Chelmsford City ground on Saturday. The Home Guard side included several Chelmsford City players, and the Navy also had some professionals in their ranks.

McLuckie also played a match for a Football League XI at Portman Road versus an Eastern Command side. Among his teammates was Preston North End's Bill Shankly. Other teams would play matches at the ground throughout the war, even though Ipswich Town would not. Although Jimmy McLuckie played three games for Town in the 1945/46 season, he retired to become a scout. The club made him redundant in 1947 and he went on to become player-manager at Clacton Town.

Other Ipswich Town regulars who served in the armed forces at this time included Tom Brown (an Army commando), Tom Fillingham, (Squadron Quartermaster Sergeant, Army), Ambrose Mulraney (Flight Sergeant in the RAF), Jimmy Wardlaw (RAF), George Price (Royal Navy), Jack Connor (RAF) and Bob Smythe (Army). Hugh Knight, a member of the office staff, was, like Fred Chadwick, captured by the Japanese in Singapore.

Only one member of the Ipswich Town staff lost his life during the Second World War. Chairman Ivan Cobbold was killed when he was attending a service at his regimental chapel in London and it was hit by a V1 bomber on 18 June 1944. He had rejoined the Scots Guards, having served with them in France during the First World War, and according to his friend and *The Times* obituarist, Lord Cranworth: 'when killed was employed with the American forces in a post of supreme importance for which he was ideally qualified'.

Ivan Cobbold was undoubtedly a key figure in the history of Ipswich Town Football Club, but has his influence on the development of the club been overstated? It seems clear that there were other figures involved in both the move towards changing from an amateur club to a professional one and the campaign to enter the Football League, such as Leonard Thompson and Nat Shaw, although his approval was certainly influential.

Following his death, a series of Cobbold family members took on the role of club chairman, starting with Ivan's uncle, Philip Cobbold. After Philip died suddenly at Christmas 1945, he was succeeded as chairman by a relative, Peter Chevallier, managing director of Fisons and a member of the family that owned the Aspall cider company. A Cobbold still remained on the board – Philip's son Alistair took Peter Chevallier's vacant place.

After the war, Town's squad was depleted and several players were brought in from other clubs as 'guests'. This arrangement often suited both club and player, as many footballers remained in the forces for some time after hostilities ceased and they could play for a club near to where they were stationed. Wing-half Harry Baird first played for Town as a 'guest' when he was stationed nearby, as did Albert Day and Tommy Parker, who was based at HMS *Ganges* and became one of Ipswich Town's best-loved players. Parker, a former railway clerk who had played rugby for England at schoolboy level, would become Alf Ramsey's first captain at Ipswich Town and would help lead the club into what was to be a remarkable period in its history.

4

Work

For a county town, Ipswich was always small by national standards. In 1871, according to the official census, there were 42,821 people living there. Gloucester, the urban centre of a similarly rural county, had a population of 534,320. As the administrative centre of Suffolk and a major East Anglian port, Ipswich was at the heart of an area that was almost completely devoted to arable farming. However, the reputation of Ipswich as being predominantly agricultural is misleading. Although much of the town's industry was related to the rural economy, nineteenth-century Ipswich was far from a sedate country town. It had plenty of heavy industry, and with it the concomitant pollution and areas of great poverty and social deprivation.

The area that immediately surrounded the town was almost completely devoted to the production of crops. In many ways, the way of life in Suffolk remained unchanged throughout the centuries until the 1960s. Many people were still employed on farms or related occupations, often living in tied accommodation. As a consequence there remained, perhaps, a certain amount of deference towards landowners and employers who had great control over the lives of their employees.

Although Ipswich Town now draws its support from all over the county and beyond, it was unlikely that was the case in first half of the twentieth century. Long working hours, lack of transport and low wages would not have made it easy for an agricultural labourer from rural Suffolk to travel to Ipswich to watch a football team, even if he had wanted to. It is likely that anyone involved or interested in football at that time would have supported a more local team. Until the advent of mass communications, such as radio and television coverage and improved transport links, combined with increases in leisure time and a greater disposable income, particularly among young men, Ipswich supporters would have mostly come from the town and its immediate environs.

Manufacturing in the town was closely related to the agricultural needs of the surrounding rural area; brewing was a major industry. Suffolk had a reputation for producing the finest quality barley and the availability of malted barley and pure water at Holywells made Ipswich a prime site for beer making. The agricultural revolution of the eighteenth century had seen several enterprising makers of agricultural tools grow into engineering firms of international reputation. An industry based on the manufacture of coprolite (fertilisers extracted from fossils) was also important to the Ipswich economy. The extraction process had been patented by the Revd John Henslow, a clergyman at Hitcham who also happened to be a professor of botany at Cambridge University. The resulting industry formed the basis of what would become Fisons Ltd.

The most common occupations in late nineteenth-century Ipswich were in brewing, engineering and industries related to the port, including a small amount of shipbuilding, mainly of sailing barges. It is hard to imagine now, but there was a regular route via the River Orwell by sea for goods and passengers between London, Ipswich and up the River Gipping to Stowmarket. The railways would eventually supersede sea travel as a method of transport between Ipswich and the capital.

The forty years preceding the foundation of Ipswich Association Football Club saw massive changes in Ipswich: the coming of the railway and the building of the Orwell Works. This was the heyday of the firm of Ransome's, later known as Ransome's, Sims and Jeffries, agricultural engineers who were a major employer in the town for two centuries. The company won an international reputation with the development of the steam engine and a steam-driven plough that was exported to Egypt for use in the cotton fields.

In the late nineteenth century, there were four other iron founders in the town, four artificial fertiliser manufacturers, fourteen corn millers and fifteen corn merchants. E. R. & F. Turner, internationally known milling engineers, set up their Greyfriars' Ironworks on what is now Cardinal Park right in the centre of Ipswich. By 1878, they were exporting their machinery to countries as far away as Hungary.

The workers in those industries would have had few hours of leisure time for playing or watching sport, but this was changing. On 10 April 1878, *The Times* reported on the progress of The Factories and Workshops Bill, then going through Parliament, which consolidated:

no fewer than 45 acts which have been passed in the course of the last 50 years. Its provisions cover nearly the whole industrial life of factory workers. The sanitary condition of factories and workshops, the fencing of certain machinery ... the hours during which young children and women may be employed, the time for their meals, the holidays which they must receive, the hours of compulsory attendance at school...

The legislation of 1878 greatly restricted the hours that children were allowed to work – children under ten were no longer allowed to work at all – and reduced the maximum number of hours that women could work to fifty-six hours per week. This may not seem relevant to the development of football as a national spectator sport, but it was part of a change in social attitudes that placed importance on the health and welfare of working people. The new law gave working people rights for the first time: the right to limited working hours and, in effect, the right to some leisure time, a new concept in its own right.

It was during this period that factory workers began to have Saturday afternoons off, and the right to holidays meant that working people were able to attend football matches as spectators. The 1850 Factory Act had specified that all work would end on Saturday at 2 p.m., which is one explanation why football matches in Britain traditionally started at 3 p.m. on a Saturday afternoon – at least until the advent of Sky Sports coverage.

The first-ever Bank Holidays were granted by an Act of Parliament in 1871. They were Easter Monday, Whit Monday, the first Monday in August and Boxing Day. The 'holy days', Christmas Day and Good Friday, had long been accepted as days off work by tradition. At first, these new holidays only applied to bank employees, as the name suggests, but in 1875 further legislation extended the right to a day's holiday to other workers.

According to Walvin in *The People's Game* (1994), at around the same time, workers' wages improved to the extent that many of them had 'a little spare cash':

> It is clear enough that more and more working men had spare money to spend as they wanted. The history of football and other organised sports shows that armies of them chose to spend some of that money on leisure.

Whether that money was 'spare' or those working men chose to spend it on pleasure rather than essentials is arguable, but there is no doubt that in the second half of the nineteenth century working men did increase their spending on leisure activities, and this would have been just as true in Ipswich as it was elsewhere.

There has been from the outset a close relationship between Ipswich Town and local industry; from the early involvement of the Cobbold family, who moved their brewery to the town from Harwich in 1746, to the present owner,

Marcus Evans, who has absorbed the club into his global operations, running what his website marcusevans.com describes as 'a global, multi-faceted, media, corporate marketing, and information company, employing 3,000 professionals in fifty-nine worldwide locations'.

Ipswich was a centre of the malting industry in the eighteenth century and the Cobbold family began as maltsters in the town. Malting locally grown barley for beer-making became such a thriving business that grain had to be imported from outside Suffolk and the Cobbold family are believed to have cornered the market in London; as ships sailed direct from Ipswich along the coast to the capital, they were in a prime location.

In 1723, one of the family, Thomas Cobbold, started brewing at Harwich but was unable to find a satisfactory supply of water, so what became known as the Cliff Brewery was founded at Holywells. In 1850, local historian and reformer John Glyde wrote:

> The supply of water to the town is mainly derived from a number of springs ... The supply is, at the present period, in the hands of nine proprietors, viz: the corporation, Messrs Cobbold, Orford, Alexander, Fonnereau, Leverett, and Smyth, the St Clement's Water Company, and the trustees of St Margaret's Charity ... Mr Cobbold's 'water-heads' supply about 600 dwelling houses. They are situated at the back of the Holywells gardens, at an elevation of 70 feet above low water mark. Some fine springs near Downham Reach Farm, the property of Mr Cobbold, are collected into reservoirs, but are only used by that gentleman for the purpose of his brewery.

In 1822, six members of the Cobbold family had joined with other bankers and businessmen to form the Ipswich Gas Light Company and the railway line through the town was built largely due to the efforts of John Chevallier Cobbold, a local Member of Parliament and magistrate. Cobbold was Mayor of Ipswich between 1842 and 1843. He entered Parliament as one of two members for following the 1847 general election and held the seat until he was defeated in 1868. The Cobbold family were also ship owners, coal and corn merchants, in effect having an interest in almost every facet of Ipswich's business and political life. Involvement with the football club was, perhaps, a logical extension of this, but it is also true that the public schools to which the Cobbolds chose to send their sons, such as Charterhouse and Eton, favoured association football over rugby. Several members of the family played for Ipswich in the early days. A relation, William Nevill Cobbold (1862–1922), whose nickname was 'Nuts', was described in his *Times* obituary as 'the most famous association football forward of all time', although he doesn't appear to ever have had a direct connection with Ipswich Town Football Club.

As well as owning a brewery, the Cobbold family were landlords. In the poorest part of Ipswich, St Clement's parish, they owned nineteen houses in the dilapidated area below New Street and around Fore Street and Long Lane. The family also rented out two shops, a lodging house on Pottery Street, and some maltings in this parish. Their biggest influence on the development of Ipswich, however, was through their ownership of a large number of pubs and beer shops. They possessed properties such as The Ship in Back Hamlet, The Grapes in Woodhouse Street, The Chequers in New Street and The Sorrel Horse on Fore Street.

The Cobbolds were major employers in Ipswich from the late nineteenth century until the brewery was sold to Ridley's in 2002. Along with other employers, such as the gasworks and Packard's manure works, the Cliff Brewery operated a 'wage ceiling' of around £1 a week, which was hardly a living wage at that time. The Cobbold connection with Ipswich Town Football Club is, of course, well documented. As we have seen, that connection began with T. C. Cobbold, the first president of the amateur Ipswich Association Football Club, and was maintained throughout the long period that led to Ipswich Town achieving professional status and entry into the Football League, only ending with the retirement of Patrick Cobbold as chairman in 1991, three years before his death.

The Cobbold family 'looked after' many of the players away from the football pitch. Apart from giving some players work when football stopped for the duration of the war in 1939, others were helped out after retirement. Tommy Parker, for example, was asked by John Cobbold to run the Magpie in Stowmarket when he finished playing, but he also worked for many years at the club's development manager and was responsible for fundraising mainly by means of raffle tickets and bingo games. In 2009, Tommy's widow, Kath, said:

> He was not just a great player for our club, he also played a vitally important role over many years behind the scenes raising large amounts of money to help Town move forward to where it is now. In a way his whole adult life was based around Ipswich Town.

Recently, Len Fletcher recalled his former teammate: 'Tommy was a lovely man. Everything revolved around him.' The same has been true of many players over the years, of course, and even now many former players, such as John Wark, Simon Milton, Russell Osman and James Scowcroft, continue to make an important contribution to the club behind the scenes.

Ipswich has been perceived as a relatively unindustrialised town, compared with the more 'traditional' footballing towns of northern England. In the 1970s, manager Bobby Robson from Newcastle upon Tyne complained that 'there are no chimney pots in the North Sea', which has been taken to mean that the working-class crowds in the industrial north were more noisy and passionate than the notoriously quiet East Anglian fans (although it doesn't quite make sense, as Newcastle upon Tyne is just as much of a North Sea port as Ipswich). In fact, the proportion of the male working population of Ipswich that was categorised in the lower two social classes (semi-skilled and unskilled manual workers) was one third in the late nineteenth century, declining to a quarter in the early twentieth century. This included people in domestic service, transport and clerical occupations, but a large number of Ipswich workers were employed in engineering, brewing, fertiliser (later agro-chemicals) production, tobacco processing and the docks. None of these industries were particular pleasant or easy. Even by Robson's time, although the number of semi-skilled workers had declined, the percentage of unskilled labourers in the town remained at around 25 per cent and this was still the case as late as 2001.

The period that immediately followed the Second World War was one of austerity (food rationing only ended in 1954) and reconstruction. The government banned midweek football matches, as they were thought to be disruptive to the productivity of workers, and in Ipswich factory hours were staggered in a number of industries, meaning that some supporters had to work on Saturdays. Many players had to wait several years to return from military service abroad or to be 'demobbed' – that is, discharged from the armed forces. Some never really recovered from their wartime experiences, like former prisoner of war, Fred Chadwick, and Herbert Clements, who had played for Ipswich in 1938, but died from heart failure, thought to have been the result of an air raid. In addition, although National Service ended for women with the war, it continued for men until 1960, with all men having to serve in the armed forces for eighteen months from 1947, unless exempted for health or other reasons. This would later rise to two years' compulsory service.

Len Fletcher, who played for Town under Scott Duncan and Alf Ramsey, recalls how he used to return from Hanover, where he was stationed following the Berlin airlift, on special leave to play for Town. Born in London in 1929, Len was brought up in Wallingford, Oxfordshire, where Robert Talbot was one of his teachers. Talbot, an Ipswich supporter and uncle of future Town midfielder, Brian Talbot, had convinced the young Leonard Fletcher that there was only one club to play for, and that was Ipswich Town. When he was finally 'demobbed' on 5 November 1949, he travelled back from Germany by ferry to Harwich and then went down to Liverpool Street station by the boat train, where he found manager Scott Duncan waiting for him on the platform with professional forms.

Billy Baxter had already signed for Ipswich Town in June 1960 when he was called up for National Service. He served with the Royal Engineers and played for the British Army side. He was still in the forces when Ipswich Town won the Championship in 1962.

Some players came to play for Ipswich as a result of their National Service. Larry Carberry had been apprenticed as a sheet-metal worker in his native Liverpool before being conscripted. He was brought to the attention of Alf Ramsey when he was stationed at Bury St Edmunds. A former Ipswich Town player told me that '90 per cent' of professional servicemen who were called up for National Service immediately after the war opted to become 'Bevin Boys', that is they worked in the coal mining or other essential industries, but most of them, in fact, worked above ground in administrative or other roles.

The second half of the 1940s saw a rapid development in professional football, including great strides in the development of youth football and an interest in a more 'scientific', rigorous approach to fitness and training. Many trainers, and indeed a large number of the players, had spent the war as Physical Training Instructors (PTIs) in the armed forces, and they were keen to try out the knowledge and techniques they had acquired. In 1949, Town brought George Smith in from Queens Park Rangers. He only appeared in eight games as a player, but he became assistant manager and a coach. It was an exciting appointment and Smith was full of ideas, introducing training sessions for local youngsters and innovative ideas about fitness. Town were having a poor season, affected by having an ageing squad and being unable to field a consistent team. They had brought in Smith, who had made one international appearance for England against Wales at Ninian Park in 1945, and he had taken over the Ipswich captaincy from Dave Bell. The move had failed to produce the desired improvement, however, and Smith, whose ideas were very different from Scott Duncan's and who appears to have provoked resentment among some of the older players, like Harry Baird, was sacked in January 1950. Alistair Cobbold, now club chairman, following the resignation of Peter Chevallier, put out a statement to the effect that Smith's contract had been terminated 'on the grounds of his misconduct and breach of disciplinary rules at the club'.

Although Smith's departure appears to have entered the club history books as a resignation, this was far from the case, and the ruthlessness with which he was dismissed echoes the treatment of Mick O'Brien. His 'misconduct' had been to write a piece for the local football newspaper, the *Green 'Un*, in December 1949 that was critical of Scott Duncan and the board of directors. Smith was clearly unhappy about his treatment by the club, because he appealed against his sacking to the Football League. He lost, as the *Derbyshire Daily Telegraph* reported on 18 January 1950:

Mr F. Howarth, the Football League secretary, announced to-day that
the appeal of George Smith against the termination of his contract with
Ipswich Town had been dismissed. The Appeals Board, consisting of
three members of the Football Association, meeting in Sheffield to-day,
upheld the League's earlier decision supporting the Ipswich club in
their action.

During the professional era, it was still necessary for footballers to have
other means of earning a living. Professional footballers' wages were not
high, particularly before the maximum wage was abolished in 1961. In the
immediate post-war period, players earned between six and eight pounds
during the playing season. Len Fletcher, who had played for both the England
and Great Britain sides at youth level in 1947, had signed his first contract
starting on a weekly wage of £6 8s, and he was paid more during the season
than in the summer: 'Scott Duncan was a shrewd operator who didn't offer
a salary increase every year. Players like Dai Rees and Tommy Parker went
pea picking and strawberry picking, to earn money during the summer.'

Post-war players were not satisfied with their low wages, however, as
they felt that they hardly reflected the revenues coming into clubs through
gate receipts. A football-starved nation packed the grounds in the years
that immediately followed the war. Ipswich Town's reserves were attracting
crowds of over 8,000, and in the 1946/47 season, over 20,000 watched a
5-0 thrashing of Norwich City at Portman Road. Nationally, the players'
union was trying to raise professional footballers' earnings – something
which they achieved in 1946 when the Football League reluctantly agreed
to an increase to £10 in winter (from £8) and £7 10s in summer (from
£6). Following the threat of a player's strike in the following season, the
maximum wage went up to £12 (winter) and £10 (summer).

The maximum wage did not apply in Scotland. When Len Fletcher
was transfer listed by Ramsey in 1955, he was offered £100 per week
by Falkirk. At the time his contract meant that he was paid £12 a week
at Ipswich, so it was hardly surprising that he accepted the offer without
any hesitation. Ten years later, in the 1964/65 season, Jimmy Leadbetter,
one of the players who had been instrumental in the side that had won
the Championship in 1962, signed a new contract earning himself £25 a
week, rising to £35.

Many players therefore had to work elsewhere as well as play
football, apart from the casual labour on the land many of the players
did to supplement their incomes during the summer. Most players, unlike
today, had worked in other occupations before they became professional
footballers. Basil Acres, who was from a relatively poor background (his
father was a part-time cobbler), seriously debated whether he should

sign a professional contract or stay working for Brantham Plastics. Some players, including Acres, also stayed on to work for the club when they finished playing. Tommy Parker, for example, spent many years as Development Manager, although he and his wife also ran the Magpie pub in Stowmarket. David Best had a complete change of career after retiring from football when he became a policeman.

Even as recent a player as Micky Stockwell (1985–2000) became a kitchen fitter. It would not be very long after his retirement from football, however, that newly promoted Ipswich Town would be paying its Premier League players tens of thousands of pounds a week.

5

Scott Duncan

When football resumed after the Second World War, the authorities made some changes to the way that the game was run. The rules were also amended so that professional footballers were allowed to play for the nearest team, with the permission of their parent club. This enabled Ipswich Town to use a number of 'guest players', several of whom would sign for Ipswich long term, including Harry Baird, Albert Day, Ian Gillespie and Tommy Parker.

Harry Baird was born in Belfast in 1913, and before the war had been caught up in a dispute between the Football Association of Ireland (the Republic of Ireland) and the Irish Football Association (Northern Ireland). He was eligible to play for both and chose the FAI, despite being threatened with suspension by the English Football Association if he did so. He was brought to England to play for Manchester United by Scott Duncan, but moved to Huddersfield Town in 1938 and guested for several teams during the war, including Ipswich – by coincidence, he was stationed with the Army at Saxmundham – and Scott Duncan must have relished the chance of bringing him to the club. He signed for Ipswich Town in 1946 and played as a wing-half, making 216 League appearances before retiring in 1952, after which he worked for the club as a coach between 1951 and 1953. He died in 1973, aged fifty-nine.

Albert Day, a striker from Camberwell in south London, had played for Brighton and Hove Albion before the war and was a guest player in 1944/45. He joined Town for a 'signing-on fee' of £300 in the 1946/47 season and he was the top scorer in that campaign, with fourteen goals in twenty-five appearances, but left for Watford on a free transfer in June 1949.

Plymouth-born Ian Gillespie played for Ipswich for a short time, making six appearances between September 1945 and May 1947. Before the war he had played for Norwich City, and after he left Ipswich Town Football

Club, he played for Colchester United and was a player-coach at Leiston from 1948. He died in Ipswich in 1988.

Of all the post-war guest players, it was Tommy Parker would make the most impact. He would have a long and successful career for Ipswich Town, both as a player and later running the club's fundraising activities. He first played for Town as a guest when he was stationed at Shotley with the Royal Navy. During his first season for Town, he remained in the navy and thus had to play as an amateur, signing as a professional footballer for the 1946/47 season. Originally from Hartlepool, where he was born in 1924, Tommy would make 465 appearances for Ipswich Town and score ninety-two goals. He was evidently a great leader on and off the pitch, frequently described in match reports and by teammates as 'pivotal' or 'central'. In his time, he held the record for most appearances made by an Ipswich Town player. When Ipswich Town Football Club won the Third Division (South) championship in 1954, a local reporter wrote, 'Full praise must be given to Parker as captain of the team. A greater captain Ipswich never had. His wholehearted endeavour and infectious enthusiasm won him the hearts of all. Here was a player who could turn a match on his own. While his team might be drooping in despair, Parker, with refound energy, would drive himself forward despite the other teams single-handed.'

Despite having been in the Football League for eight years, the 1946/47 season would only be Town's second full campaign. The highlight of the season was almost certainly a 5-0 thrashing of Norwich City at Portman Road in front of a crowd of over 20,000. Albert Day got a hat-trick and Tommy Parker scored two goals. Ipswich also won the away fixture at Carrow Road, this time only 0-1. It was a promising comeback after such a long break and Ipswich Town finished sixth in the Third Division (South).

Town made a remarkable start to the 1948/49 season by winning the first three matches, 6-1 away at Bristol Rovers and two successive 5-1 victories at home to Torquay and Newport County. A major contribution to their good form was the introduction to the side of Jackie Brown, a Northern Ireland international. Brown signed for Ipswich when he was thirty-three years old, and had already played for Wolves, Coventry City and Birmingham before the war. Despite his age, he had a successful career with Ipswich Town, and was highly regarded. Described in several match reports as 'orchestrating' the side, he made a total of 103 appearances and scored twenty-seven goals.

Unfortunately, the sixth game of the season was against Notts County at Meadow Lane. The hosts had – surprisingly – acquired the England centre-forward Tommy Lawton from Chelsea in 1947. It was almost unheard of for a player to choose to drop down to the Third Division from a top-flight club, but Lawton had fallen out with the Chelsea manager,

Billy Birrell, and he had worked with the Notts County manager, Arthur Stollery, before when he had been a physiotherapist at Chelsea. It was certainly a coup for County and it brought them success.

County won 9-2 and Lawton, 'on international form', scored four goals. The *Western Daily Press* reported, 'Ipswich were completely outclassed and could not counter brilliant approach work in which Lawton was always the leading figure'.

Lawton was a superlative player, but the nature of the defeat also demonstrated how old the Ipswich side had become. The combined age of the team that played Notts County was 362 years. Full-backs Dave Bell and George Rumbold were thirty-eight and thirty-seven years old respectively, and central defenders George Perrett, thirty-three, and Matt O'Mahoney, thirty-five, were not much younger. Harry Baird, Jackie Brown, John Dempsey and Jackie Little were also over thirty. Only the goalkeeper, Tom Brown, and forwards Tommy Parker and Bill Jennings were in their twenties. Of course, this was mainly because the six years of war had disrupted the natural progress of younger players, but nevertheless it was beginning to have an effect on the team.

Ipswich did well to finish seventh in the Third Division (South), but the following season went badly. Not helped by the dismissal of 'go-ahead' trainer, George Smith, who had introduced innovative coaching methods, fitness regimes and pressed for the younger players to be brought through, Town were bottom of the League at Christmas 1949 and finished the 1949/50 season in seventeenth place. They conceded ninety-six goals in forty-seven matches (in all competitions) including losing 6-0 at Watford and 5-0 at Aldershot.

Scott Duncan's reputation for being 'careful' with money is likely to be partly due to stereotyping owing to his Scottish origins, but he was certainly not profligate when it came to spending money on transfers. Duncan was an administrator who dressed like a bank manager and had indeed been a legal clerk before joining his local team, Dumbarton, playing as an outside-right. Described as 'shrewd' and 'canny' by people who knew him, Duncan was reluctant to involve Ipswich Town in the growing fashion for spending big in the transfer market. 'In these days of fantastic transfer fees,' he said, 'fancy figures are not necessarily the hallmark of a good player.'

The 'fantastic transfer fees' that Duncan was talking about seem quite low in these days of multi-million-pound players, but he was astute in pointing out the rapid rise in the level of transfer fees at that time. Amounts paid for top footballers would continue to grow and become a problem for the less wealthy clubs. The pre-war record had been £14,500, which Arsenal paid Wolves for Bryn Jones in 1938. Tommy Lawton, who had put four goals past Town for Notts County in 1948, had been transferred from

Chelsea for a then record fee of £20,000. In 1951, Sheffield Wednesday paid Notts County another record fee of £34,000 for Jackie Sewell.

Defeats on the pitch forced Duncan's hand. He brought Allenby Driver in from Norwich City for £3,000 and Jim Feeney (the father of future Northern Ireland international, Warren Feeney) and Sam McCrory came from Swansea City for a combined fee of £10,500. In addition to this, Vic Snell was signed from a local club, the Nicholians, without a fee. Neil Myles and John Elsworthy, who was playing as an amateur at Newport County when he signed for Town in May 1949 also arrived at the club. Elsworthy would go on to become a stalwart of the Ipswich side that won the Division One title in 1962.

A new trainer also arrived at the club to replace George Smith. Jimmy Forsyth, nicknamed 'Chisel', would remain at Portman Road until 1971 and work under five different managers.

Despite the new faces, Ipswich made a slow start to the 1950/51 season, only earning five points from the first six matches. However, there were improvements, and they finished the season eighth in the League. More importantly perhaps, the days of conceding large numbers of goals appeared to be over, the only thrashings being meted out were by Town, who beat Gillingham 5-1 and had revenge on Aldershot by defeating them by five goals to two.

Duncan again brought in fresh players during the summer, and by 1952 the average age of the squad had dropped dramatically. In January of that year, they fielded a side where every player was under thirty. Remarkably, this was the first time it had happened in the history of the club. Town's forty-three-year-old goalkeeper, Mick Burns ('a brilliant man ... a very fit man', according to Len Fletcher) had played in the 1937 cup final for Preston North End, but was now beginning to give way to Jack Parry who had been signed from Swansea City for £750. Another younger player was Basil Acres, a local player from Brantham, who was aged twenty-five.

Financial problems meant that the some of the players that Duncan had brought in would depart relatively quickly. Regular goalscorers, Sam McCrory, Allenby Driver and Jimmy Roberts were all transferred out. Sam McCrory went to Plymouth Argyle for £6,000 – a move that angered many supporters, who considered it to be a derisory amount.

Subsequent seasons brought more problems. Town's poor form had resulted in attendance levels falling to as low as 3,116 for a match against Leyton Orient in March 1953. The club needed to draw crowds of around 12,000 and was beginning to make serious financial losses on a regular basis. A spate of injuries to other key players such as Tom Garneys and Dai Rees, plus serious flooding at the ground, all conspired against Town both on the pitch and in financial terms.

At the end of the 1952/53 season, Town finished a poor sixteenth in the League. It was one place above where they had ended the previous season, but with everything that was going on at the club, it must have felt as if Town was on a downward trajectory.

It was all the more remarkable, then, that the 1953/54 season would see Ipswich Town win the Third Division (South) championship shield. They made a brilliant start to the season, their first defeat only coming in their eighth game away at Reading. In fact, they remained unbeaten in all competitions in thirty-two matches, losing only once more (to Queens Park Rangers) before being again beaten by Reading on 23 January 1954. A blip in February and March 1954, when they lost six out of their nine League games and an FA Cup match, meant a more tense finish to the season than there should have been. Injuries to players and a good Cup run took its toll. Town reached the fifth round of the FA Cup, losing to Preston North End, a team that featured both Tommy Docherty and Tom Finney, in front of 34,500 spectators at Deepdale. With nine games remaining until the end of the season on the 1 May, Ipswich looked as if they were going to be beaten to the title by Brighton and Hove Albion, but Town didn't lose another game, winning seven and drawing twice.

Tom Garneys scored twenty-four goals that season. Nineteen were in League matches, including six vital goals during April 1954. Garneys, from Leyton in east London, had started his professional career at the relatively late age of twenty-five because of the war. He signed for Ipswich from Brentford in 1951 for a transfer fee of £2,700 and became one of the club's most popular strikers – a crowd chant of the time was 'Give it to Garneys'. He went on to have a successful career under Alf Ramsey until he retired in February 1959. In later life, he ran a sweet shop in Queensway, off the Nacton Road and, for some years, was the landlord of the Mulberry Tree in Woodbridge Road.

Duncan had brought other players in, partly because the team had been hampered by player injuries. Billy Reed, George McLuckie, and Alex Crowe turned out to be inspired choices.

Billy Reed came from promotion rivals Brighton and Hove Albion for a fee of £1,750. A right-winger, who could dribble the ball brilliantly, Reed would make a massive contribution in the 1953/54 seasons. He was described as 'the Stanley Matthews of the Third Division' – praise indeed at a time when Matthews was generally regarded as being the best player in England, if not the world.

George McLuckie, described as 'a gem of a man' by someone who knew him in later life, was not related to Jimmy McLuckie, the star player before the Second World War. Originally from Falkirk, he came to Ipswich from Blackburn Rovers in May 1953 and so his first season with the club was one in which he won promotion. A winger, he scored twelve goals in fifty-three appearances in 1953/54, and a total of twenty-five goals in 125 games between 1953 and his transfer to Reading in 1958.

Alex Crowe, another Scot, came from St Mirren and played a crucial role in that promotion season. He would only stay at the club until 1955. Another signing that season was Ted Phillips, who was spotted playing for his local side, Leiston. Phillips would remain with Ipswich until 1964 and become a Town legend.

The promotion party was huge. Club captain, Tommy Parker, was presented with the Third Division (South) shield at Portman Road following the final game of the season against Northampton Town on 1 May 1954. The *Evening Star* match report two days later described the scenes:

IPSWICH PLAYERS 'MOBBED' FOLLOWING FINAL VICTORY

The final chapter to Ipswich Town's triumphant season was written at Portman Road on Saturday. Ipswich, who had already made certain of the championship ... beat Northampton Town by 2-1 before a crowd of 22,136.

Of the game itself the spectators probably cared only little. They were at Portman Road to witness an occasion - one that was without parallel in the history of the club and ... few would have missed, not even for the Cup Final; for some who had obtained tickets preferring to see Ipswich.

Although the result was of no great consequence, it was important for Ipswich to win. If Northampton had taken both points or even forced a draw the after-match scenes would have seemed somewhat false. As it was Ipswich got home for their 27th win of the season and thus finished three points ahead of Brighton and Hove Albion.

For Ipswich it was a game with a difference, and afterwards the players were agreed upon the fact that there had been an atmosphere all of its own. Even three-quarters of an hour before the kick-off there was a pent-up expectancy amongst the spectators. The 'cheer leaders', if they may be called such, paraded the touch lines. They wore blue and white favours, carried swedes on long poles and indulged in good natured banter with the crowd.

A mighty roar greeted the Ipswich team when they ran on to the field and a dozen large blue balloons appeared as if from nowhere and drifted across the pitch. Twenty minutes before the end of the match the fun started again.

As soon as whistle sounded the crowd rushed the pitch. Northampton fled from the scene and Ipswich to the comparative safety of the enclosure.

Formal proceedings over the police tried to form a tight circle around the players and shepherd them across the field ... however ... Parker was at last hoisted shoulder high and borne from the field. Other players were also 'chaired' and as the heroes vanished from sight the crowd sang 'For they're all jolly good fellows'.

Celebrations had already taken place after the team had arrived back from beating Newport County 2-1 on 26 April and were greeted by a huge crowd of supporters at Ipswich railway station. They toured the town centre in an open-topped bus and the Supporters' Association hosted a small party at Portman Road. Following the final game, the bus tour was repeated, this time with the trophy to show off the Third Division (South) Championship Shield and a civic reception was held at the Town Hall. It is unlikely that many of those present would have dreamt that there would be many similar celebrations on the Cornhill to come in the second half of the century.

Promotion to the Second Division was to be the crowning glory of Scott Duncan's career at Ipswich Town, but it did not last. Town did not survive their first season there and were relegated, ending the 1954/55 season in twenty-first place. Nevertheless, Duncan can be credited with consolidating the club financially (the promotion season brought the crowds back to Portman Road and presumably also helped to refill the club's coffers) and established a decent Football League side that would become a contender in future campaigns. Scott Duncan should be remembered as one of the most important Ipswich Town figures for those reasons, although it is likely he came to the club – leaving a similar role at Manchester United – because the board of directors had offered him a massive salary, thought to be £2,000, making him one of the highest-paid figures in football. To give a little perspective, the average male wage in 1937, the year Scott Duncan came to Ipswich Town, was £201.60.

Scott Duncan's time at the helm saw the club make a great move forward and begin to establish itself in the Football League and look like a side that was going places. Shrewd, a tough negotiator and an effective administrator, he was according to his assistant, Pat Godbold, 'A *secretary*-manager, with the emphasis on secretary.'

Despite his conservative appearance and manner, it seems that Scott Duncan was quite a character. Pat Godbold tells a story how on one occasion, John Cobbold caught him watering down the whisky in the referee's room. Referees weren't paid at that time, they just received expenses and a few drinks. When John Cobbold protested at the sacrilegious act being committed by his manager, Duncan replied, 'Don't worry about it. It's only for the bloody ref!'

According to Len Fletcher, 'Scott Duncan didn't pick the team ... or, at least, only on occasions...' The directors would watch the Tuesday morning practice match and then, 'after the directors had been on the Friday, the team sheet would come out'. One of the directors who was most interested in on-field matters was Ernie Steel. 'He was a great judge of a footballer ... not skills-wise, but in [judging] their appreciation of Ipswich Town.' Scott Duncan resigned as manager in 1955, following relegation back to the Third Division (South) but he would stay on for a further three years, working as club secretary alongside the new boss. When Alf Ramsey arrived as manager in 1955, he picked the team.

6

Places

Broom Hill and Brook's Hall

Portman Road has been the home of Ipswich Town since 1888, when the association football club merged with Ipswich Football Club, the local rugby team who had been playing there since its formation in 1870. The ground was owned by the Ipswich Corporation, and it remains in the hands of Ipswich Borough Council at the time of writing.

Before 1888, however, Ipswich Association Football Club played at two adjacent sites on the outskirts of Ipswich, Broom Hill and Brook's Hall. On 17 October 1878, the *East Anglian Daily Times* announced the club's official debut, 'The first game was fixed for Saturday week, on the club ground, at Broom Hill, Norwich Road, at 3 p.m.'

Broom Hill, now usually known as Broomhill Park, appears to have already been in use as the Ipswich AFC ground by the time that first game was played. The local press certainly always referred to it as the 'Club Ground'. It was not used exclusively by Ipswich Association Football Club, however. Several other local teams, most notably the Orwell Works' side, which had its home at Brook's Hall right next to the Broom Hill ground, also used it. In fact, it seems that many match reports used the names of the two sites interchangeably and somewhat confusingly. Rugby was also played at Broom Hill, including an annual match between Orwell Works and the London club, Clarence. The park was additionally used for charity matches and schools' events, where a range of sports including cricket and football were played.

The reason that the association club started its life at Broom Hill becomes obvious once it is known that the land was privately owned, and the owner was founder member and player, George Sherrington. It was in a part of Ipswich known as Brook's Hamlet, also spelt Broke's or Brooke's in older documents. This was the site of a medieval moated manor house, which was mentioned in the Domesday Book, but the building was long gone by the time the place was being used for football. Sherrington's mother's maiden name was Brookes and it may not be coincidental. Ownership of the land might well have inherited through her family. Sherrington would sell the land to the Borough Council in 1925. A small area of parkland, known as Sherrington Road Park, remains in that part of Ipswich today and football is still played there.

Broom Hill itself was a hilltop covered with woods, and appears to have been quite unsuitable for football. The area is now in an urban part of north-west Ipswich, but would have been on the outskirts of the town in 1878. Brook's Hall (now the area around Westwood Avenue) was land immediately to the south of Broom Hill and the home for a long time of the Orwell Works Football Club. Match reports from the early years of Ipswich Association Football Club are full of complaints about the sloping, poorly drained and difficult conditions of the playing surface there, one commentator even referring to 'the mountain ranges and morasses' of Brook's Hall.

The changing rooms at Broom Hill in the early years of Ipswich AFC were basic, at best. It is thought that players changed in some kind of hut or 'lean-to' shelter, and by the club's Annual General Meeting on 5 September 1881, the subject of dressing rooms had become a serious issue. The committee and the club's new secretary, Henry Peecock, were set the task of finding ways of improving the facilities. It appears that the solution had been to arrange for the players to use the yard at the back of the Inkerman public house on the Norwich Road. For several years, this was where players changed after games, using a cold water pump there to clean themselves up.

By the 1882/83 season, Ipswich Association Football Club was playing many of its games at Brook's Hall. It's quite likely that the two grounds were, in fact, next to one another, and the names often appear to be used interchangeably in match reports. The site had no permanent floodlights. The famous match held under 'electric light' in December 1878 was played on the Brook's Hall site, but the lighting had been brought in for the occasion. It had been illuminated by 'Electric machines ... supplied by Mr Paterson, of London and driven by two of Messrs Ransomes, Sims and Head's portable engines (kindly lent for the occasion).'

Matches may have been played at Broom Hill under moonlight, however. Ipswich footballer, Ernest Kent described moonlit matches that were played in Ipswich in the 1880s in one of his 1906 articles for the *Evening Star*. Conditions in these games were hardly ideal, either for the players or the spectators, as play could only go ahead if there were cloudless skies, fine weather and a full moon.

The first game that Ipswich Association Football Club played at Brook's Hall was against Framlingham College and took place on 26 March 1881. It appears that Broom Hill continued to be used for 'practice matches' or friendlies. Brook's Hall was still the venue for Orwell Works' matches, and Ipswich Association had to take second place to that team and were unable to play if Orwell wanted to use the pitch. This was probably one of several reasons why Ipswich AFC began to gravitate towards the idea of playing at Portman Road at this time, along with the poor facilities.

Ipswich Association Football Club played at Portman Road four times in the 1885/86 season in the Suffolk Challenge Cup, and may have been impressed with the difference between the flat pitch there and the sloping ground at Broom Hill/Brook's Hall. It is clear from the Suffolk Football Association's choice of Portman Road as the venue for its cup finals and other major events that it had already become the premier football ground in the county by the end of the 1880s.

At the club's Annual General Meeting on 18 September 1888, chairman Stephen Notcutt told members that the tenancy of Brook's Hall was insecure and they could be given as little as one week's notice to quit. The pressure for development of that part of Ipswich because of the growing industrialisation in the town may well have been a contributing factor too, but presumably this didn't apply to Broom Hill because the Sherringtons owned it and it doesn't seem as if they had any plans to sell at that time. It would appear that the most pressing reason for the amalgamation of the association club with the declining rugby club was the desire to move to its headquarters to the better facilities and central location at Portman Road.

Portman Road

Ipswich Association played its first ever game at Portman Road in a benefit game against a local side, The Pilgrims, on 15 January 1884. However, the team continued to play at either Broom Hill or Brook's Hall until 1888 when the association and rugby clubs amalgamated and agreed to share the ground at Portman Road, at first playing on alternate Saturdays. Football matches were then played on what is now the training pitch in an east-west direction immediately behind where the west stand, currently called the East of England Co-operative Stand, was built many years later.

Other sports events, such as cycling, were also held at the ground. There was no seating. Supporters stood a few rows deep around of the pitch, the perimeter marked by a single rope. At this time, football matches were played across the area where the practice pitch is now. Since 1855, the ground had also been used for cricket during the summer and the East Suffolk Cricket Club played there. Other sports, such as athletics, tennis, cycling, and hockey, would continue to be played on the 'old' ground. This groundsharing arrangement lasted until 1891, when the rugby club left Portman Road for good. From that point onwards, Portman Road has been the home of Ipswich Town Football Club.

On 18 November 1891, Town played a side of Canadian and American touring side, the first ever game against a 'foreign' team. The North Americans were at the end of a very long and exhausting itinerary of exhibition matches and Ipswich won 2-1. The tourists wanted a fee of £20, but the gate receipts failed to cover that amount.

It was partly the fact that Ipswich Town's committee still clung to their ideas of amateurism that prevented the development of the ground. Portman Road would be behind other grounds for many years to come. The changing rooms at this time were basic. The team was supposed to use the cricket pavilion at Portman Road, but many players preferred to go up to the Station Hotel to use the facilities there. The secretary, Philip Cornell, believed that the club could not build permanent structures, including stands, because they were tenants of the Corporation. Boards were laid around the touchline for spectators to stand on, and in 1897 the press were finally able to use Portman Road's first 'media centre' when a hut was built at the side of the pitch and a table provided for reporters to sit at.

At that time, at the behest of the cricket club who were concerned about their pitch, the football field was moved so that it ran from north to south (it had previously been laid out in an east-west direction). There continued to be tensions surrounding footballers damaging the cricket square, however, and in 1890 the football pitch was moved to its current location. At the time, this was an area of marshy wasteland, with poor drainage that has continued to prove a challenge to the ground staff ever since. It makes their achievements all the more laudable. The pitch at Portman Road was frequently praised by visiting teams and the reporters in both the local and national press from an early date.

When Aston Villa came to play a Suffolk County side at Portman Road in 1898, a temporary stand was erected on one side of the ground and wagons were drawn up to enable the large crowd of 5,000 to watch the match. Plans were underway to build a grandstand, but it was not until the 1904/05 season that the club were able to make significant improvements to the ground. It was at that time that the Ipswich Corporation – the future Ipswich Borough Council which owned (and still owns) Portman Road – agreed to have an area of wasteland next to the ground levelled to provide an improved pitch to be used exclusively for football. In June 1905, the Corporation renewed the club's lease on Portman Road for a further twenty-one years and later that year, in November, the Ipswich

Cricket, Football and Athletic Ground Company Limited was formed with capital of £2,000.

During that period, Portman Road saw other changes, including the construction of the Churchman's tobacco processing factory on the south side of the ground in 1901. This, and other developments in the area around the ground, must have changed the environment quite dramatically. Up to that date the ground had been surrounded on three sides by trees and must have had quite a rural feel to it, but the monolithic and rather unprepossessing factory came to dominate the skyline for many years to come and, of course, the south stand was (and for many still is) known as Churchman's because of it.

The grandstand was finally constructed in the 1906/07 season by the local building firm of W. G. Fisk & Co. It cost £230 to build. Fisk's may have made a good job of building the stand, as it lasted for decades in one form or another, but it didn't stand up to a severe gale on 6 November 1911. The high winds took the corrugated metal roof completely off and the sides of the grandstand, which were made of glass, fell inwards and the substantial repairs that were necessary cost the club a further £60. At the same time, a 7-foot-high fence was built around the ground to prevent those members of the Ipswich public who hadn't paid the admission fee of sixpence seeing any of the play. Given that the 1906 Wage Census put the average male weekly wage at between 28s 6d and 29s 6d, sixpence would have been quite an expense for the average working-class supporter.

The following season, 1907/08, a new cricket pavilion was built. It cost a little more to build than the grandstand, £280, and was used, amongst other things, as a changing area for the players. To picture the scene at Portman Road in the period leading up to the First World War, it is necessary to imagine a single grandstand on the east side with the rest of the ground lined with around 2,000 people standing along the boundary ropes. By the early 1920s, whippet racing had been added to the various events that were held at the ground.

In 1921/22, there were further disagreements with the Corporation, leading to the suggestion that the club would move away to a new site at Belvedere Road. In the event, whatever the dispute was, things settled down and Ipswich Town remained at Portman Road. The disagreement between the club and the Corporation may well have been connected with the amount of rent that the Corporation wanted to charge. At least, a few years later, in 1927/28, the rent went up to £500 for the season. Conditions, however, appear to have still been poor. In 1926, for example, a home game had a delayed start while rats were removed from the grandstand. A further stand was built in 1928/29 on the west side of the ground. This would develop over the years to the Pioneer Stand and is now the East of England Co-operative Stand. It was a small stand to begin with, and without a roof, but for the first time the seats were numbered and members of Ipswich Town Football Club were each allocated their own seat.

Once again, in 1936, a move away from Portman Road was proposed, this time to the Suffolk Greyhound Stadium owned by one of the club's directors, Nat Shaw. This was part of the campaign for the club to turn professional and it was suggested that even the supporters of rivals Norwich City might be enticed away to watch Ipswich Town there, although this seems unlikely as the Norfolk club were no longer playing at The Nest, but at their own brand new ground at Carrow Road, which was built in 1935. The plan for the redevelopment of the greyhound track, which reached an advanced stage, would have increased the stadium's capacity to 30,000 with seats and covered stands.

The resolution to become a professional football club, which was passed during a meeting at the Town Hall on 1 May 1936, specified that the new Ipswich Town Football Club Ltd would play at Portman Road however, and a further commitment to remain was demonstrated by the renewal of the ground's lease for a further twenty-one years. This time the Corporation would charge the club £120 a year for the first seven years, rising to £150 for the middle period of the lease, and to £200 for the last seven years. This would mean that the club would remain where it was until 1957 at the earliest, and presumably put an end to the speculation about moving to the greyhound stadium.

Subsequent development must have given a greater sense of permanence too. Iron railings were put up around the pitch, replacing the rope around which generations of spectators had gathered to watch sport, and goalposts were set up – Town had been one of the first clubs to put nets between the goalposts in 1890. The terraces at what became known as the North Stand were roofed and 'banked', that is, built up in a gradient – in that era this was normally done using rubble from construction sites and railway sleepers. 650 tip-up seats were bought from Arsenal and installed in the grandstand. The Churchman's end was partially covered at a cost of £1,450. Other improvements included painting the ground blue-and-white and the installation of stoves to heat the dressing rooms in the pavilion. The football club, and the recently formed Supporters' Association, were investing in order to create an infrastructure that would stand them in good stead in this new, professional era to which they aspired and to accommodate the larger crowds that would hopefully arrive if Town were elected to the Football League.

Further improvements followed the club's successful bid to join the Football League in 1938, including the addition of extra turnstiles. Churchman's was upgraded so that the stand ran along the whole width of the pitch. The first

Football League game at Portman Road was against Southend in front of a crowd of 19,242 spectators. Ipswich Town would now be playing regularly in front of more than 15,000 people. The record for that first season was 28,194 for the FA Cup third-round replay against Aston Villa on the 11 January 1939. Town had managed a 1-1 draw at Villa Park (in front of 34,901) and brought the Villans back home, but unfortunately lost 1-2.

The admission price for matches was increased to a shilling at this time. Money was taken on the turnstiles and collected by assistant secretary Donald Read at half-time. Read was usually accompanied around the ground by a policeman and two other members of the club's staff.

The ground had not been requisitioned by the War Office during the Second World War, and unlike in 1918, League football resumed at Portman Road as soon as the war ended, although the Third Division (South) was further sub-divided, probably to save on travelling. Petrol rationing didn't end until 1950. It was therefore in the Third Divisions South (North) that Ipswich Town began the 1945/46 season and, after two away matches, the first fixture at Portman Road was on 1 September 1945 against Port Vale. Town lost 0-1.

A record League crowd of 20,267 football-starved supporters watched a game against Queens Park Rangers on Boxing Day 1946. In the same year, the grandstand roof was again destroyed by gale-force winds, which lifted it off completely and left it in the cattle market (now the car park) nearby. Throughout this period, the Supporters' Association continued to raise and donate money to pay for repairs and the development of the ground. The Supporters' Club was pivotal during the 1950s, for example, when Town was on the verge of bankruptcy and donated £3,000 to pay for work on the terracing of the new West Stand, which was completed in 1952. Two years later, the Supporters' Association once again raised the money to pay for new terracing in the north end. Capacity was increased to around 29,000 by 1956.

There were few major structural changes at Portman Road during the Ramsey era, despite the success on the pitch, but small improvements were made continuously, often paid for by the Supporters' Association. These included the construction of a central section of the West Stand with some seating at the back and a further extension at the sides of that stand, which brought the seating capacity up to almost 2,500. The total capacity of the ground was by then 31,000. A public address system was installed, and in 1959 the first floodlights were put in place, costing £15,000. They were officially switched on by Blanche Cobbold, widow of Ivan, before a friendly against Arsenal in February 1960.

Success on the pitch meant that improvements to the roofs of the stands and the terracing continued throughout the 1960s. The Supporters'

Association supplied the £35,000 required for improvements on the North Stand in 1963. An administration block was added in 1965, and in the same year proper dressing rooms were built at the corner of the West Stand and Churchman's. Incredibly, it appears that players were still using the old pavilion to change up to this date.

In 1967, more turnstiles, including some separate entrances for young people, were added at the Churchman's end. There had been a campaign by a group of parents demanding that 'juvenile areas' to be set up. There is no record of the reasons for this sudden parental concern, although a good guess might be that it was because of the colourful language of some members of the crowd.

The following year, a ninety-nine-year lease was granted by the Borough Council, but it was conditional upon major development work being carried out at Portman Road within twenty-one years. The capacity of the stadium had already increased, by degrees, to around 31,500, which consisted mostly of terraces for standing in only, which was normal at the time. There were plans to add another 5,000 places to the Churchman's Stand.

In this period, according to Simon Inglis, author of *Football Grounds of Britain* (1983), 'Ipswich emerged under Bobby Robson as one of the country's most successful teams, [while] Portman Road was transformed into one of the best grounds.' Plans were made towards the end of the 1960s to erect a new stand on the east side of the ground – what would eventually become the Cobbold Stand. This would finally replace the old 'chicken run', parts of which still dated back to the early years of the twentieth century. It was finally taken down in 1971 and most of the old stand was moved to the speedway stadium at Foxhall Road, where it was used until 1987. A new grandstand, at first called the Portman Stand, which had seats for more than 3,500 spectators, as well as terracing, was constructed. It had cost £180,000 to build and the ground's capacity would now be around 37,000.

The new grandstand was officially opened by Sir Alf Ramsey before the home game with Everton on the first day of the 1971/72 season. The huge financial investment necessitated that, for the first time at Portman Road, advertising boards were put up around the perimeter of the playing area and the pitch was moved (and the width was cut by 6 feet) to accommodate this. The extension to Portman Road's capacity resulted in the home attendance record being broken several times in successive seasons, including in the League games against Manchester United (31,918) and Arsenal (34,196). Crowds of over 30,000 turned out quite regularly for the 'bigger' fixtures.

Autumn 1974 saw further building on the Portman Stand, extending it to run the length of pitch at a total cost of £500,000. This meant an additional 1,600 seats. By 1975, the extended Portman Stand was now fully open and a ground attendance record of 38,010 was set at an FA Cup 6th Round match against Leeds United. The capacity of Portman Road had reached approximately 38,600. In 1977, the club spent £300,000 to again increase the capacity of Churchman's and replace the old wooden steps and terracing at the back of the stand. The roof of that stand was also extended with crush barriers and extra turnstiles also added.

Ipswich Town continued to develop Portman Road in 1978 with the construction of twenty-four executive boxes in the Portman Stand. These would be available for three-year periods at a cost of £5,000. The standing area in front of the boxes was replaced by 1,800 seats, taking the capacity of the ground down slightly to 34,600. A further six executive boxes were added to the Portman stand in 1980 and the wooden benches in the West Stand were replaced by plastic seats. The following year it was renamed the Pioneer Stand with 4,800 seats, following a sponsorship deal that would enable the club to build a completely new stand that was used from the 1982/83 season. It ultimately cost £1.4 million, and was officially opened by the Minister for Sport, Neil McFarland, with Suffolk-born former FIFA President Sir Stanley Rous and the Cobbold family in attendance. Sir Standley was born in Mutford, near Lowestoft in 1895, went to school in Beccles and had long-standing connections with Ipswich Town Football Club.

By this time, the club's fortunes seemed to be on the wane again. In the season that Ipswich, under manager Bobby Ferguson, were relegated back to the Second Division, average attendances fell from well over 17,000 to 14,452. This meant that there was a fall in ticket money coming into the club too, leaving Ipswitch with debts.

In the last two decades, development at Portman Road has been largely governed by the recommendations of the Taylor Report of 1989/90. The report was the result of an official inquiry into a tragedy at Sheffield Wednesday's Hillsborough ground, in which ninety-six people died and 766 were injured. The Taylor Report changed the way that football supporters would watch their sport dramatically, and one of the most significant effects was the move to end standing at football matches completely. In 1990, Ipswich Town Football Club spent £105,000 making the Pioneer Stand into an all-seater section. In the summer of 1992, the club did the same to the Churchman's end and, perhaps more controversially, the North Stand, the traditional 'stronghold' of the Ipswich faithful. As Simon Inglis wrote:

Compared with the antipathy and drawn-out anguish experienced by other clubs, it was perhaps typical of Ipswich to have made the transition in this fashion [that is, the decision was made as a *fait accompli* and the supporters came back to an all-seater stadium at the start of the 1992/93 season], and typical of Ipswich fans largely to accept the sudden loss of their terraces with such calm resignation.

Portman Road became (at a cost of £550,000) the first all-seated Premier League ground with a new, lower, capacity of 22,438. Not all fans did accept it, however. Some have never returned to Portman Road since.

Following a return to the Premier League, when Ipswich Town beat Barnsley in the First Division play-off final at Wembley in May 2000, there was rapid development of the ground driven by the chairman, David Sheepshanks. The North Stand was rebuilt in 2003, leaving a gaping hole at one end and a similar void in the Portman Road atmosphere that didn't help their chances of staying in the top tier in what was to prove a difficult second season in the Premier League. The *Architect's Journal* of December 2003 described the new stand:

> Ipswich Town Football Club's new North Stand at its Portman Road ground seats more than 7,000 fans – 4,000 more than its predecessor – with vastly improved facilities including a club superstore, bar, WCs, lifts and staircases to provide easy access for all, including wheelchair users.

It also required the club to borrow £22 million, and was the beginning of a long period of financial troubles following relegation to the First Division, which included briefly going into temporary administration. The south stand was also redeveloped later and both stands were eventually formally renamed in honour of the club's greatest two managers. The North Stand became the Sir Bobby Robson Stand, shortly after his death from cancer in September 2009, and the old Churchman's end at the south of the ground officially became the Sir Alf Ramsey Stand in March 2012, on the fiftieth anniversary year of the club's First Division championship.

Both of Ipswich Town's great managers have been honoured by Ipswich Town supporters in the form of two life-size bronze figures. The first, a statue of Sir Alf Ramsey, was commissioned by the Ipswich Town Supporters' Club following a suggestion by Seán Salter, a supporter and member of the Supporters' Club management committee. Sir Alf Ramsey's image was cast in bronze by another Ipswich Town supporter, artist Sean Hedges-Quinn. It shows Ramsey in a characteristic pose with one hand in his pocket and it has become a popular meeting place for home and away fans. It was unveiled at a simple ceremony in August 2000 by Sir Alf's widow, Lady Victoria Ramsey. The Ipswich Town Supporters' Club chairman, Philip Houseley, told the media that they had received 'the encouragement of Lady Ramsey throughout the whole project'.

The £25,000 cost of the statue was met by the Football Association, Ipswich Town Football Club, Ipswich Town Supporters' Club, Ipswich Borough Council, the *Evening Star* newspaper and a number of private donations. The unveiling was attended by many of Ramsey's former players from both his time at Ipswich and as England manager, including Sir Geoff Hurst and Sir Bobby Charlton. On the same day that the south stand was named after Sir Alf Ramsey, the six surviving members of his Championship-winning side, Andy Nelson, Larry Carberry, John Compton, Doug Moran, Ray Crawford and Ted Phillips, laid a wreath in his memory at the statue.

It soon became apparent that many of the club's supporters felt that there should also be a similar statue to Sir Bobby Robson, who was sixty-nine years old by this time and had recently been knighted. He was able to be present at its unveiling in July 2002, typically commenting that he felt 'overwhelmed. Proud and ever so slightly embarrassed. Deeply honoured.'

The statue was again the creation of Sean Hedges-Quinn, and this time was funded by the Supporters' Club, the Borough Council and the club's main sponsor at the time, TXU Energi. When Robson died on 31 July 2009, the statue became the focal point for a huge outpouring of grief from supporters of Ipswich Town and many other clubs. Flowers, scarves and other memorabilia were placed around the statues and festooned the blue railings for the entire length of the stadium – almost, as one newspaper suggested, turning it into a shrine. Nothing could have demonstrated the emotional attachment that Ipswich Town supporters have for the memory of Sir Bobby Robson, the history of the club and the place that Portman Road has in their hearts more distinctly.

Football supporters are attached to the physical places that they associate with their clubs; sometimes they even get married at football grounds or have their ashes scattered or buried there. In an interview with the *East Anglian Daily Times*, Town legend Kevin Beattie, who was brought down from his Carlisle home at the age of fifteen by Bobby Robson, revealed that it would be his dying wish to have his ashes scattered at Portman Road. 'I love Suffolk,' he said, 'and will never, ever move away. When the big man up there decides that my time has come I want my ashes scattered on Portman Road in the four corners of the ground – north, east, south and west – just to say The Beat is still here.'

It is this almost religious sense of place that makes a football ground so important in the hearts and minds of a club's supporters. Their shared experiences go beyond what happens on the pitch and, in this increasingly secular world people are often brought together as a community in a way that is no longer possible in churches, mosques or temples. In December 2006, 25,000 football supporters stood for a minute's silence at Portman Road in memory of five young women who had been brutally murdered in or near the town. The Right Reverend Richard Lewis, Bishop of St Edmundsbury and Ipswich, led prayers and a minute's silence that was observed by the visiting Leeds United fans in the Cobbold stand. Other clubs, including Leeds United, have had their own tragedies, but this was an example of Ipswich supporters being drawn together as a genuine community at a very dark time.

The importance of the places associated with Ipswich Town, and Portman Road has been connected with it even before it became its official home in 1888, is only matched by the sense of attachment that the club's supporters have to those places and to the football club that they love.

7

Alf Ramsey

The resignation of Scott Duncan at the end of the 1954/55 season meant that, for the first time since 1937, the club had to look for a new manager. At thirty-five years old, Alf Ramsey had reluctantly retired as a player. He'd had a successful career as a right-back for both Southampton and Spurs and had been an England international 1948–53. He had been overlooked for a coaching role at Tottenham, and many people were surprised when he was appointed as manager of lowly Ipswich Town.

However, Ramsey had connections with the East of England. He was born in Dagenham, which was then a small village, in 1920. Dagenham was in a rural part of Essex at that time. It would develop rapidly in the late 1930s when it was designated a 'new town' and a massive programme of public housing was undertaken to house people living in the slums of London's East End. The Ramsey family was poor or, as Alf would put it, with characteristic understatement, 'We were not exactly wealthy.' His father was a labourer who picked up work when and where he could get it as a dustcart driver, a hay and straw dealer, and eked out a subsistence living for his family on a smallholding. The Ramseys were believed by some people to have been of gypsy origin and his nickname when young had been 'Darkie'. Yet there is no evidence that Alf's family were gypsies or travellers. His paternal grandfather was from Levington in Suffolk and his great-grandfather was from Martlesham. His mother's family, the Bixbys, came from Dagenham and Barking in Essex. All were labourers, mainly working on the land. They moved around within Essex and Suffolk frequently, as did many people. Times were hard and labouring-class people had to move to where the work was.

Ramsey was coaching in Rhodesia (now Zimbabwe) when Ipswich Town approached him about the manager's job. Having been appointed on 9 August 1955, he at once made a good impression on supporters and members of the local media alike. The *East Anglian Daily Times* reported that, 'Mr Ramsey's views on the press and football are such as must gladden the heart of a reporter,' and he wrote to the fans in the Supporters' Association Handbook for that year, 'I sincerely hope that our association will be a happy and successful one. In the past you have supported the club one hundred per cent and I would like to feel that in this, my first year as manager, you will do the same.'

In the summer of 1955, Scott Duncan had signed Jimmy Leadbetter from Brighton and Hove Albion for £1,750. It was another astute move on the part of the retiring manager and Leadbetter, a talented winger, proved to be a great asset for his successor. Ramsey brought in some new players himself, but made it known that he would give the existing squad a chance to prove their worth. An injury to goalkeeper Charlie Ashcroft, in March 1956 (he had only arrived from Liverpool in June 1955) forced Ramsey to bring in Roy Bailey only two days before the transfer deadline expired. Bailey was playing for Crystal Palace at the time and living in a caravan in Lewisham.

Town's regular goalkeeper at that time was George McMillan, but Bailey soon took the number one position permanently and would go on to win the Third Division (South), Second Division and First Division titles with Ipswich. He retired to South Africa, where he coached the national side and became a well-known media figure. His son Gary, also a goalkeeper, would play for Manchester United and England. Roy Bailey would be another piece in the jigsaw in what was arguably Ipswich Town's most successful League side.

Despite losing his first game as manager at home to Torquay United, Ramsey would have an immediate impact on the side. After beating Southampton in the second match of the 1955/56 season 4-2 (again at home), Town had an impressive run, beating Swindon Town 6-2, Walsall 5-2, Millwall 6-2, Reading 5-1, QPR 4-1, Northampton Town 5-0, Millwall (away) 5-0 and Norwich City 4-1. They ended the season in third place, but the change in the style and quality of football under Ramsey quickly attracted the attention of the media.

In an article entitled, '"Thinking" Sides Score Heavily: Signs of More Imaginative Approach in League Football', on 5 September 1955, *The Times*' Association Football Correspondent reported that 'there were healthy contributions of six goals each from West Ham United and Ipswich Town (now managed by the thoughtful Ramsey)'.

The presence of a manager of Ramsey's stature drew unprecedented attention to Ipswich Town and, following his first season at Portman Road, a considerable amount of anticipation. The 1956/57 season began badly however. Town lost its first three games, including losing badly (1-4) at home to Torquay United. The recovery was due, in large part, to the skills of a Suffolk-born player, Ted Phillips.

Phillips had been spotted playing for his home-town club, Leiston, and signed for Ipswich in December 1953 season, but had presumably – and inexplicably, given his subsequent reputation – not made much of an impact. He had been sent out on loan to Stowmarket Town for most of the 1953/54 season. In 1956/57, Phillips scored a remarkable forty-six goals in forty-four appearances, including an average of one goal in every League match that he played in. Notorious for the net-bursting power of his shots on goal, he scored five hat-tricks in that season, contributing to the team's final tally of 128, including 101 goals in the League. It was hardly surprising that Ipswich Town won the Third Division (South) again, although this time they only did so by beating Torquay on goal difference.

Town's 2-0 defeat of Queens Park Rangers at Loftus Road on 16 March 1957 made the headlines for another reason, as the *West London Observer* reported a few days later:

> There were wild scenes at Loftus Road when a spectator attacked Mr B. A. E. Buckle, who was in charge of the game against Ipswich Town on Saturday. When the game ended the referee had to be escorted to his dressing-room, and large crowds awaited his departure from the ground, but he was escorted away safely from another exit.

The match report describes what was quite an even game, but Queens Park Rangers lacked the ability to finish. The crowd had booed the referee throughout and presumably their tempers got the better of them after two late Ipswich goals, shortly followed by the referee 'taking the name' of one of their players, George Petchey. This provoked a Rangers' fan to run on to the pitch and hit the referee. Earlier the same season, on 5 January 1957, Ipswich Town had been reprimanded by the Football Association for similar behaviour (but not violence) by spectators at Portman Road towards the referee after he blew the whistle disallowing a last minute equaliser against Fulham.

Once again, crowds celebrated Ipswich's promotion to the Second Division at Ipswich railway station and around the town, although, possibly because of the experience of promotion a few years before, the festivities seem to have been more muted. *The Times* noted events briefly, adding 'the success of Ipswich is the culmination of a remarkable recovery, reflecting particular credit on the former England full-back, Mr A. Ramsey, in his second season as manager'.

Under Ramsey, Ipswich did better on their return to the Second Division and they finished in eighth place. It's only possible to speculate how well the club might have done that season if Ted Phillips had not been out for most of it through injury and illness, including having to recover from a cartilage operation. He only played eleven games, but continued his remarkable strike rate by scoring eleven goals. This was a period of consolidation for Town, and despite the acquisition of Ray Crawford from Portsmouth for a transfer fee of £5,000 and the return of Phillips in the second half of the season, they finished the 1958/59 season in sixteenth place. Ray Crawford would become one of the most popular players in Ipswich Town history. A prolific centre-forward, he scored twenty-six goals in thirty-three appearances in his first season, a standard that that he kept up consistently throughout his career at the club. His overall record was 227 goals in 353 games.

By the start of the 1960/61 season, Ramsey had managed to go a long way towards building the squad that would bring him his greatest success at club level: Roy Bailey, Billy Baxter, Larry Carberry, Ray Crawford, John Elsworthy, Jimmy Leadbetter, Andy Nelson, Ted Phillips, Derek Rees and Roy Stephenson would all be key players for him. The side that Ramsey put together and would eventually win the First Division championship cost a total of £30,000. He brought in talented unknown players, like Baxter who had been scouted when playing for Broxburn Athletic, a Scottish amateur side, and still had his National Service to do when he joined Ipswich. The combination of the wingers Leadbetter and Stephenson, who could put precise, diagonal balls in to Crawford and Phillips, transformed the side. The fact that both strikers were available for all forty-two games was vital to the team's successful campaign. Scoring exactly 100 goals in Division Two in the 1960/61 season, Town were promoted as champions. They had made sure of promotion on 22 April by beating Sunderland 4-0 at Portman Road, but a 4-1 win against Derby County at the Baseball Ground meant that they could afford to lose their final game against Swansea and still be at the top of the League. Ipswich Town had finally reached the highest level of English football.

This was not only a period of massive development in the material side of Ipswich Town Football Club, but also one in which, under manager Alf Ramsey, the club would achieve greatness for the first time. 'First Division football has reached East Anglia at last,' trilled *The Times* on 24 April 1961. 'Ipswich Town joining Sheffield United in promotion with a wide victory over Sunderland can now prepare to face an entirely new life among the upper classes.' It was presumably in response to remarks like this, alongside predictions of a single season in the top tier and the label of a 'Cinderella' club, that, the very upper class, chairman John Cobbold made his famous riposte, 'Cinderella is getting quite a big girl now, isn't she?'

Two days earlier, a 4-0 win over Sunderland in front of over 21,000 spectators had assured Town of promotion and, although there were two more games left in Division Two that season and they would only be promoted as champions the following Monday, when they beat Derby County at the Baseball Ground, the faithful were able to celebrate at home. Town were two goals up at half-time (Elsworthy 4, Crawford 38) and emotions were already running high enough for Ramsey to speak to the crowd over the public address system, asking them not to run on the pitch at the end of the match.

Crowds during that season had averaged 15,095, but it should be remembered that the entire population of Ipswich was only around 100,000 at this time.

Town must have dumbfounded those commentators who forecast that Ramsey's side would fall straight back down into the Second Division by winning the Football League championship in the following season. This time the press took notice. On 29 April 1962, the *Sunday Pictorial*, the precursor of the *Sunday Mirror*, whilst not failing to refer to the club as 'Cinderella', ran a banner headline 'CHAMPION, IPSWICH' and enthused alliteratively, 'Sensationally, staggeringly, stupendously, the championship of the Football League came to rest proudly in the sunny flat farmlands of Suffolk last night', then went on to describe events at Portman Road:

> Picture the tumultuous scenes at the end. Five minutes after play had ceased a calm loudspeaker announcement revealed the amazing news that Burnley had dropped a point to Chelsea and given the title in Ipswich.
>
> Jubilant, joy crazy, backslapping, fans invaded the pitch. They clamoured for their heroes to return.
>
> Slowly, a little sheepishly, came the reluctant heroes of the under-rated Ipswich. Hundreds mobbed the players. Forty-goal hero Crawford, was hoisted on ten broad shoulders.

Reporter Sam Leitch appears to have been left with only the haziest memories of the match itself and apologised for not reporting its details, continued to effervesce: 'Bottles of champagne ... trainer Jimmy Forsyth thrown fully dressed into the Ipswich bath ... and Burnley chairman Bob Lord phoned his congratulations...'

Photographs of the pitch invasion show the players running off the pitch to escape excited young men, wearing duffle coats and rosettes, but they are familiar scenes of celebration, despite the different clothes and haircuts, to those that have taken place at Portman Road since.

On the following Monday, *The Times* even used John Cobbold's Cinderella joke as its headline adding that 'Ipswich [was] perfectly drilled by 'the General'. *The Times'* Association Football Correspondent was more circumspect than his red-top colleague when he described events at the end of the match, but continued the romantic and fairytale theme:

> Soon the 30,000 crowd broke like a dark wave over the greenest pitch in all the land; the players, called from their humble dressing room, did a lap of honour almost embarrassed by all the attention; and an incessant chant rose for the man who had quietly planned this remarkable feat in the background – Mr Ramsey.

One little known incident was recalled by Mike Langley, a reporter of that time, who wrote an affectionate memoir of Sir Alf in the *Guardian* on 1 May 1999 after Ramsey had died on 29 April. He wrote mostly about his time as manager of England and his treatment at the hands of the FA, but referring to the 1961/62 season said:

> The final great journey of that championship year was to London and the Savoy, but not just the team, their largely Old Etonian directors and sundry civic dignitaries. Alf, with that firmness which brooked no argument, informed the board: 'This championship was everyone's success, so everyone comes. If they don't, I won't go.'
>
> So all 28 players on the books were invited, including the aptly named reserve Kenneth Stiff. Also the groundsman and his assistant Stan Prendergast. The office staff as well. Alf, and this was his secret with England after Ipswich, overlooked nobody. Unity was his game, and so the Savoy played host to old-age pensioners who swept up at the ground.

In twenty-five years, Ipswich Town had moved from being an amateur, non-League club to the top flight. It was a remarkable achievement, and even the rather patronising comments in the media were accompanied by genuine admiration. Town's arrival in the First Division coincided with another monumental development in English football. In January 1961, following a campaign led by Jimmy Hill, chairman of the players' trade union, the Professional Footballers' Association, the maximum wage (then £20) was scrapped.

The Times of 18 August 1961, greeted 'a changed world where the British professional player of the leading echelons at last finds himself a member of the upper income group able now to earn anything between £2,500 and £4,500 a year for nine months of service'. In the same column, the writer added, 'While welcoming Ipswich Town to the First Division for the first time one cannot but shed a little tear to find Newcastle, Preston and Portsmouth mixing in the servants' hall. It is all part of the new age, no doubt.'

The press predicted that Ipswich Town would have a short stay in the First Division, but then the most optimistic supporter would have hesitated before thinking that Alf Ramsey would take the club from the Third Division to be champions of the Football League in so short a time.

The formidable pairing of Ray Crawford and Ted Phillips was once again crucial. In 1961/62, Crawford made forty-one appearances in the First Division and scored thirty-three goals. Phillips did only slightly less well with twenty-eight goals in forty League games. This was even more impressive given the quality of football teams they were playing against. They included George Cohen and Johnny Haynes for Fulham, Geoff Hurst and Bobby Moore for West Ham and Matt Busby's Manchester United (who Town beat 4-1 at Portman Road), featuring Bobby Charlton, Nobby Stiles and Johnny Giles.

The press began to admit that Ipswich Town were, in fact, able to compete with the best:

That Ipswich are a welcome addition to the First Division there is no question. Their football is thoughtful, simple, relaxed, as indeed one might expect from pupils of Mr Ramsey ... Birmingham will not be the last city-slickers to leave this homely rural scene with a lungful of invigorating Suffolk air as the only reward for their labours. (*The Times*, 11 September 1961)

Ipswich won the First Division title on 24 April 1962 in front of almost 29,000 ecstatic supporters. In that season they had beaten Manchester United, Chelsea, Aston Villa and Arsenal.

Despite his amazing success, Ramsey was not without his critics at Ipswich. Ernest Steel, a long-serving member of the board of directors, resigned after complaining that Ramsey was 'negligent' and the other directors were a 'bunch of Ramsey's yes-men'. This seems a little harsh, given what Ramsey have achieved at the club. Town were only the second club after Wolverhampton Wanderers to win the Third, Second and First Division championships. Wolves have taken thirty years to do it, whereas Ipswich under Ramsey had taken six.

The *East Anglian Daily Times* paid tribute to Ramsey:

The Town's triumph is his and his alone ... He cares deeply for the footballers in his care and knows far more of their capabilities and limitations than they know themselves and we have seen them blossom and react to his coaching. Completely unemotional, never over-excited or deeply depressed, he has performed a modern miracle in football.

Much has been made of Ramsey's lack of emotion on winning the First Division championship with Ipswich, but it is not borne out by the recollections of his men. Jimmy Leadbetter thought Alf wanted to step back and let them have the limelight. 'He did not want any praise. When people congratulated him, he gave all the credit to the players.'

One less well-known (and more endearing) story, which shows Ramsey in a rather different light, is that, when the celebrations were over, John Cobbold found him sitting alone in a completely empty Portman Road, looking out over the ground. Without saying anything, Alf handed his jacket to the chairman, went down on to the pitch and did a silent, private lap of honour.

Ipswich would have a difficult second season in the First Division, finishing in seventeenth place in 1962/63. Max Marquis, in his rather sour biography of Ramsey, thought it was because other teams had been able to work out how to deal with Crawford and especially Phillips, who was only able to score nine times. His analysis is unkind, but it is probably true that Phillips had been found out to a certain extent:

> One trouble, among many others, was that before he shot, Phillips always did a little shuffle ... Phillips might as well have rung a handbell when he intended to have a crack at goal ... Defences now knew Phillips, and he was finding goals very difficult to come by. Leadbetter was injured, and Bailey was off form in goal. Ipswich's luck was running low.

Everyone who knew Ramsey describes him as a quiet and unemotional man. Pat Godbold, who worked alongside him for eight years at Ipswich, recalls, 'I didn't really get to know him. He was a very private person.' However, she also believes that despite that aspect of his character, he had an immensely strong rapport with his side. 'He wanted his players to socialise with each other, even though he didn't want to himself. If the team had a bad game, Alf would just say, "Didn't play so well today, boys."'

Another biographer, Dave Bowler, wrote:

> It was Alf who put Ipswich on the map, who gave the club its greatest triumph and he made life easier for all those who followed him to the club. He was a superb *team* manager, one of the very best ... At heart, Alf was a player's man, loved being with them, working with them.

Ramsey would leave Ipswich Town to become the greatest ever manager of England, guiding them to victory in the 1966 World Cup finals. His treatment at the hands of the Football Association is well documented, and it has cast a shadow over the reputation of one of the greatest-ever managers in English football. Hopefully, it will soon be time for a re-evaluation.

8

Home

For all that the physical places are important to Ipswich Town's story, it is the supporters that are at the very heart of the club. Although Ipswich originally would have drawn its support almost exclusively from the town, it now has a large body of fans from all over the county of Suffolk and indeed the world. The Supporters' Club has branches in countries like Italy, Norway, Serbia, the United States and Australasia. There are Norwich fans in parts of North Suffolk, and Ipswich has also drawn many supporters from Essex and Cambridgeshire. Younger fans might find it hard to believe that as recently as the 1960s, some Ipswich fans would attend home games at Portman Road one Saturday and go to Carrow Road on alternate weekends. Likewise, many people have supported both Ipswich Town and Colchester United, the towns being less than 18 miles apart.

Although the size of crowds in the nineteenth century is hard to establish, given that newspaper reports are unreliable, they would have been quite small even in the professional game. The very first FA Cup final between Wanderers and Royal Engineers on at the Oval cricket ground in 1872 attracted only 2,000 spectators. However, by the mid-1880s, League crowds at Bolton, Nottingham and Derby all exceeded 15,000 on occasions. By 1899, a pre-season match by Newcastle United was being watched by more than 20,000 people, and the 1893 Cup final between Wolverhampton Wanderers and Everton at Fallowfields in Manchester was seen by 45,000 paying spectators, although many more (an estimated 15,000 more) watched for free as crowds broke through the barriers.

It is difficult to estimate the number of spectators that watched Ipswich Association Football Club in the early days at Broom Hill and Brook's Hall. Local newspaper reports rarely commented on the size of the crowds, let alone gave accurate attendance figures. It's likely that the first game played 'with the aid of electric light' at Orwell Works on 17 December 1878 ('6*d* in advance, 1*s* on the night and 1*s* 6*d* for a reserved place') attracted a higher than average crowd, but unfortunately local newspaper reports only refer to a 'large concourse of people', many of whom would have been attracted by the novelty of electric light itself. The *Ipswich Journal*, while praising the football club for giving the people of Ipswich the opportunity to see the lights, mentions that 'hundreds' attended – presumably many more than for an average game played at Broom Hill in daylight.

Ipswich occasionally played matches in front of sizeable crowds in those early days. In March 1892, a match between one of the leading clubs, Preston North End and a Suffolk XI attracted 3,000 spectators to Portman Road. Preston were the first-ever champions of the Football League and they were also the first professional side to play at the ground – with former Ipswich star player, George Sherrington as referee. The visiting side won 3-0 in what, according to the *Ipswich Journal,* was 'a splendidly contested match ... probably the finest Association match ever seen at Portman Road.'

It was the professional teams from the Football League that attracted the largest numbers to Portman Road. A crowd of about 2,000 saw Ipswich Town beat Old Harrovians 6-2 in February 1896, and more than 5,000 people watched Aston Villa play a Suffolk County XI at Portman Road on 26 February 1898 (Suffolk lost 1-4). Such was the anticipation surrounding this match that the local railway company, Great Eastern, probably for the first time, laid on football specials to bring spectators to Ipswich from around the county. The growth in the size of the crowd at this time appears be confirmed by reports of a huge increase in gate receipts during the 1890s leading to the appointment of Ipswich Town's first treasurer.

A report in the *East Anglian Daily Times* on 4 October 1890 that described the first-ever FA Cup match at Portman Road against Reading gave no information about the attendance, but the report reveals how popular association football was becoming in the town:

The fact of this being the first English Cup Tie played at Ipswich caused an immense crowd to line the ropes all round the ground, nor had they cause to repent their coming ... The great popularity and keen interest now taken in Suffolk football was amply demonstrated on this occasion by the thousands of spectators, the gentler sex [*i.e.* women] being strongly represented.

Only a modest number 'lined the ropes' for a less attractive cup tie in the second qualifying round against Norwich Thorpe, which Ipswich won 4-0.

'Gentler sex' or not, there were reports of 'disgusting language' at matches involving Ipswich during the 1890s. Reports of bad behaviour at Portman Road are rare, and there was certainly nothing in the Suffolk press similar to this report of a crowd at a football match at Shrewsbury in 1899 (quoted in Walvin's *The People's Game*). At that time, Shrewsbury was a small town club similar to Ipswich:

> There were many thousands at Shrewsbury on Easter Monday, the concomitants of betting, drinking and bad language were fearful to contemplate, while the shouting and horseplay on the highways were a terror to peaceful residents, passing homewards.

Occasionally, there were complaints that the behaviour of Ipswich Town fans was not what it should be. A match that took place on 21 October 1893 against the Coldstream Guards drew criticism from the *Ipswich Journal's* football columnist, 'Half-back':

> The largest crowd which has yet appeared on the Portman Road ground this season witnessed the match with the 2nd Coldstream Guards on Saturday, but at the same time if it was the largest muster of spectators it was also the least orderly gathering I have seen around the ropes for a very long time. The manner in which the referee was yelled at when his decisions were adverse to their ideas of right, and their discourteous criticism of the visitors' style of play was anything but creditable to an Ipswich audience, and not only gains for the town an unenviable reputation in the football world, but also tends to keep good teams from visiting the enclosure ... The rowdyism appeared to be chiefly confined to one section of the audience, and I sincerely hope that for the sake of their own credit, and that of Ipswich Town Football Club, these excitable partisans will keep their feelings a little more under control.

In 1906, former Ipswich player Ernest Kent, writing in his column for the *Ipswich Journal,* made what was a brief reference to the spectators at those early games, 'Those matches produced many enthusiastic followers of the game – apart from the devoted band of supporters who smoked Isabellas on the touch-line, and who were no mean factors in the disputes.'

In a subsequent article, Kent complained of remarks made by people standing along the touchline to watch the game. Writing twenty years later, the irritation still shows through:

> To stand by the ropes, or even to sit on a stand, does not give one a fair view, of all the circumstances; it is not like a bird's eye view of a

chessboard. I have always said that spectators should advance their theories with much deference. Many a time have I been called names for doing this or that – or not doing it – when I have been sure that what was done was the best, if not the only, thing to be done at the moment. Since one cannot yet hover above the ground, the spectator sees a match only from his point of view.

Comments in the local press about the nature or behaviour of the people who attended matches were rare, however, apart from when applause was significant, although there were occasional reports of pitch invasions by over-enthusiastic supporters.

In January 1901, the *Sheffield Daily Telegraph* reported that 'a commission of the Football Association ... sat at Ipswich on Thursday to inquire into the alleged misconduct of spectators at a match between Ipswich Town and Kings Lynn at Ipswich, on November 8th last...' Having taken evidence from a number of witnesses, the commission announced that 'the Ipswich Town Club were cautioned as to the behaviour of their spectators and informed that it is their duty to afford proper protection for visiting teams between the crowds and the dressing room'. A comment was also made about the regrettable behaviour of spectators at football matches in Norfolk and Suffolk generally. The 'alleged incident', according to a report back in December 1900 in the *Ipswich Journal*, occurred when 'a member of the Kings Lynn team was struck by a person on the way to the railway station'.

On 5 January 1957, when Alf Ramsey was the Ipswich manager, the club were reported to the Football Association because of the misconduct of some supporters. Town were having another successful campaign – they would again win the Third Division (South) championship at the end of that season – but trouble broke out after the referee, K. Stokes, blew the whistle for full-time just as Billy Reed scored from a Tom Garney's cross. The result was therefore Ipswich Town 2, Fulham 3. A furious Ramsey went to the referee's room at the end of the match to discuss the matter and a large group of Town supporters gathered outside the dressing rooms and started chanting, 'We want the ref! We want the ref!' The Football Association required Ipswich to publish a warning about the future conduct of spectators in the official match programme.

The late 1960s and 1970s saw a long and sometimes unpleasant era of violence and hooliganism among English football supporters. In October 1968, the *Times* ran an column entitled 'Violence is all part of the game now' and went on, 'Violence, on and off the field, has established itself, rightly or wrongly, as an integral part of the current "image" of professional football, Britain's major spectator sport.'

Although references can be found to a somewhat mythical 'firm' called the Ipswich Punishment Squad, there is no evidence – apart from some graffiti – that such a thing existed and, if it did, it was certainly not comparable with some of the more notorious groups such as the Chelsea Headhunters or the Inter City Firm. Nevertheless, all supporters were affected by changes introduced to counteract football-related violence at this time, from the withdrawal of cheap fares for railway specials, to police controls of where and when fans could congregate.

Despite Ipswich fans being among the best-behaved in the Football League, local Labour Member of Parliament Ken Weetch was outspoken on the subject and, at a meeting with local police, publicans and officials from the football club in August 1975, he attempted to bring in a licensing system in Ipswich. The rather authoritarian proposal was that the coach companies that brought away supporters into the town for matches would be issued with a licence to do so only on condition that fans arrived no more than two hours before a match and would take them away again immediately after the game had finished. Weetch also campaigned for tougher penalties for people convicted of football-related hooliganism.

On Saturday 26 August 1976, twenty-six football supporters appeared in court at Ipswich following fighting on the terraces at Portman Road and a pitch invasion. According to *The Times*, 'all but three' of those accused gave addresses in London, but that, of course, doesn't necessarily mean that they weren't Ipswich Town supporters. On the same day, a seventeen-year-old boy had been stabbed to death in a game between Arbroath and Celtic in Scotland.

In May 1977, a Wolverhampton Wanderers' supporter, Gerald Comerford, was killed when changing coaches at Cambridge on the way home from an FA Cup tie at Portman Road when someone threw a 'missile' at him from a passing car. The match had been marred by violence, with nine injuries and thirty-one arrests. A sixteen-year-old boy was charged in connection with his death. In August that year, there were thirty-three arrests at a home match against Arsenal. It was at this time that Ipswich Town installed crush barriers before a home game against Chelsea. Nationally, police were asking for shields and helmets as mini-riots occurred on a regular basis at football grounds around the country.

On 23 March 1978, Ipswich fans attending a game at Millwall's ground, the Den, for an FA Cup tie were attacked before and during the match. Play was held up for eighteen minutes after the fighting spilled on to the pitch. Forty-five people, including eleven police officers, were injured and thirty people were arrested. The problems were not, however, entirely caused by troublemakers from the south-east London club. Of the fourteen supporters to appear in court at Camberwell on the following Monday, one, twenty-four-year-old David King from Trimley St Martin, near Felixstowe, was alleged to have run across the Millwall ground shouting, 'Ipswich for the Cup!' and swearing at the home fans, who then invaded the pitch. King admitted using threatening behaviour and was remanded on bail. The magistrate told him that he could expect a custodial sentence.

The Times inteviewed 'Mr Robert Robson, manager of Ipswich Town' immediately afterwards. 'To think,' he said, clearly angered by what had occurred, 'we fought in the war so that hooligans like that could survive. These people are not human and have no place in society. They will kill the game.'

The Football Association set up a commission of inquiry following this match to look into the growing problem at football matches. Chairman Sir Harold Thompson, the same football administrator who had handled the dismissal of Alf Ramsey from the England manager's post with 'brutal insensitivity', told *The Times* that he would like to see 'these people prevented from going to matches by being locked up every Saturday'. Ken Weetch called for Millwall FC to be closed down and an Ipswich businessman, Alan McCusker, started a campaign for this to happen. The group he set up planned to issue a charter to end football hooliganism and wrote to the Prime Minister, James Callaghan, 'It is vital to initiate a nationwide and co-ordinated campaign to remove the deep concern and horror of many thousands of ordinary people who feel that a near double-decade of ever-escalating violence and filth at soccer grounds, and indeed in society generally, is no longer tolerable.'

Disturbingly, football-related violence began to take on a more sinister, calculated aspect. In 1988, an undercover policeman, Michael Fickling, 'infiltrated' a gang of Leeds United supporters. In his evidence at a subsequent trial at Leeds Crown Court, he described a trip with them to Portman Road on New Year's Day 1987, saying that the group had targeted black Ipswich Town supporters and one of them, Martin Pickard, had boasted of assaulting a black Ipswich Town fan.

During the 1970s and 1980s, Ipswich had a significant proportion of black supporters, mainly from the small, but well-established Afro-Caribbean community in the town. Ipswich had benefited from immigration for many centuries, from the French and Dutch refugees of the sixteenth century to the migrant workers from countries like Poland and Portugal that make up part of its thriving community now. Fifty-two people were recorded as having been born in the Caribbean islands by the 1951 census, the majority from British Guyana, Jamaica and Trinidad. By 1961, the numbers had risen to 943 people and, of course, many of those people had settled in the town and their children were born there. By the time the 2001 census was recorded, there were 1,625 people who described themselves as black, black British or black Caribbean. In addition, an Asian community had grown by this time: 5,285 whose ethnic origin was from the Indian sub-continent and 758 Chinese people.

In the 1970s and 1980s, Ipswich's support appears to have been more ethnically diverse than it is now. Very few black faces can be seen in photographs of Portman Road crowds taken in the 1960s, but by the time Ipswich Town won the FA Cup in 1978 that had changed quite dramatically. One supporter of another club wrote in the fanzine *Those Were the Days* that his fellow fans, on a trip to Portman Road, had noticed this and started chanting 'you're just a town full of n*****s' and other offensive songs, and were surprised when the Ipswich crowd responded with 'Ipswich Town are black and white'.

By that time Ipswich Town's youth policy meant that it was quite naturally bringing through some young, talented, black local boys. Many of them would go on to become stars, including Jason Dozzell, who still holds the record of being the youngest player to score a goal in the top flight of English football. He was only sixteen when he scored for Ipswich against Coventry City on 4 February 1984. Jason, from Chantry in Ipswich, was a genuinely local product. Ipswich Town writer, Gavin Barber has described him as, 'more Ipswich Town than Ipswich Town themselves ... to the casual observer he was slow and uncoordinated. To the dwindling number of regulars at Portman Road he was indisputably a misunderstood genius.'

Dozell would play for England at under-21 level, and go on to have a rather unsuccessful spell at Tottenham Hotspur. His brother, Tony Swallow, was a well-known supporter of the club and his son, André, is currently a member of the youth academy.

Bill McGarry had brought in Town's first black player, Bristolian defender Steve Stacey. McGarry signed him from Wrexham for a fee of £25,000 in September 1968. Before he did so, he rang the offices of the *East Anglian Daily Times* and asked for an opinion on how the locals would react to him. He was told 'if he can play, sign him up'.

Stacey, who moved to Western Australian and worked for an Aboriginal sports organisation, Nyoongar Sports, remembers his time at Ipswich 'with mixed emotions'. Unfortunately, he did not have success on the pitch. Town already had a black player in its academy, John Miller. He made his first team debut in March 1969 against Coventry City and moved to Norwich City in 1974. This was a time when black players received a great deal of verbal abuse, usually from away supporters, but unfortunately, such things were not unheard of at Portman Road, although racism was neither as organised nor as rife in Ipswich as it was at some clubs. Long time supporter Alasdair Ross remembers a West Indian supporter, Goose Gladstone, leading the singing in the North stand and that visiting fans would shout abuse at him, including what are known as 'monkey chants'. His response would be to make a joke of it, and sing a song that was then famous in a television advertisement, 'Peanuts! Get jungle fresh, Golden Wonder! Get jungle fresh Peanuts! Get jungle fresh.'

Another incident recalled by supporter Stuart Hellingsworth in an article in a recent fanzine *Turnstile Blues*, describes the reactions of Ipswich Town supporters to racism and fascism:

> One Town fan was amongst the travelling blue army when an infamous fascist organisation tried to portray themselves as Ipswich fans at Highbury in the '80s. The police decided to deal with all of the Ipswich fans. Fortunately, a number of Arsenal fans stood up and informed the police that they weren't Ipswich fans but National Front. The Arsenal and Ipswich Town Football Club fans then stood together as one against the right-wing group on the terraces of Highbury. Another occasion where the National Front infiltrated the opposition fans saw the chants of 'There ain't no black in the Union Jack' met with 'Ipswich Town lives in racial harmony.'

That isn't to pretend that there have not been any problems with Ipswich Town fans and racism and, to their shame, a deeply offensive song about former Norwich City player Justin Fashanu is sometimes sung by a minority of fans.

Ipswich Town Supporters' Association

The first official Ipswich Town supporters' club, Ipswich Town Supporters' Association, began life on 24 November 1930, at the Crown and Anchor Hotel in Westgate Street. The meeting, which was attended by eighty people, had been called by Jack Eggert, who became the first secretary of the association. Murray Walker, who ran a draper's shop in the town, became the first chairman and Major Harold R. Hooper, the president.

Hooper was one of the driving forces behind the move to turn Ipswich Town into a professional club, as was Leonard P. Thompson, who with his father, Philip Webster Thompson, a builder's manager from Withypoll Street, was an early force in the Supporters' Association. Thompson became chairman of the association in 1936, by which time there were more than 1,000 members paying one shilling a year subscription. As secretary of the newly formed Ipswich Town Football Club Ltd, Thompson was also supervising building work at Portman Road, much of which would be paid for with money raised by the Supporters' Association over the years.

It is not possible to give an exact figure of what the Supporters' Association contributed over the years, but it is quite clear that supporters donated very large amounts of money towards the material development of the club, including the building of stands and other facilities. In 1967, the Association's publicity officer, Joe Gardiner, estimated that they had given approximately £240,000 in total to Ipswich Town Football Club between 1936 and 1967.

In addition to financing building work at Portman Road, the Supporters' Association acquired a house in Christchurch Street just after the Second World War, which they named after the country residence of the Cobbold family, Glemham Hall. The house was bought specifically to rent to players after Scott Duncan had commented that the club was having difficulties attracting top quality players from elsewhere because of the lack of suitable accommodation: 'We could sign a good strong player straight away if we could find an unfurnished flat.' Matt O'Mahoney, who made sixty appearances for Town between 1945 and 1949, had applied for a transfer because he couldn't find a house after his marriage in 1947. The purchase of Glemham went a long way towards resolving the problem.

By the time Scott Duncan had taken Ipswich Town up from the Third Division (South) to the Second Division in the 1953/54 season, the Supporters' Association had a membership of over 10,000. It continued mainly as a fundraising organisation, but also ran social events and acquired its own premises, the Manor Social Club and Ballroom in St Margaret's Green. In 1962, Alf Ramsey wrote to the Supporters' Association, just before the club's first season in the First Division claimed, 'Sometimes, when I look at our fixture list ... I am frightened and ask what I have done to deserve this. Then again, I think that this is something really worthwhile to fight for. We have got to improve, but I am certain that we shall improve. We have a great chance ... I think we shall show some people we are quite a team.'

Despite the Supporters' Association's generosity towards the club over several decades, divisions arose between members of its committee. They became so difficult to reconcile that during the 1966/67 season Ipswich Town Football Club announced that it would no longer recognise the Supporters' Association. Rogan Taylor mentioned the story in his book *Football and Its Fans* (1992):

This sorry tale was related to the NatFed's [National Federation of Football Supporters' Clubs] 1967 Annual General Meeting by the Ipswich Town representative:

Right: 'The past is a foreign country...' Victorians by the Wolsey Gate, Ipswich. (David Kindred)

Below: The original Tractor Boys: agricultural labourers in late nineteenth-century Suffolk. (Kingsley Fletcher)

The Ipswich School team at Broom Hill in 1887. The letters on the crest on their shirts are 'IAFC'. (Ipswich School)

The Inkerman, close to Broom Hill & Brook's Hall. Ipswich players changed in the yard during the nineteenth century. (Kingsley Fletcher)

The Cliff Brewery: the Cobbold family were patrons of the football club and local employers for many years. (Kingsley Fletcher)

Right: Claude Sennitt, who played for Ipswich between 1909 and 1912. He died from wounds received in military action in 1917. (Norfolk Library Service. Copyright: A. E. Coe Ltd.)

Below: Scott Duncan (left), with Jimmie Hogan, manager of Aston Villa, before an FA Cup third-round replay in 1939. (Getty Images. Photo by J. A. Hampton/Topical Press Agency/Getty Images).

Town players relaxing after a match, 1939. Clockwise from front left: Fred Chadwick, Billy Dale, next three are unidentified, Bryn Davies, Jimmy McLuckie, Dave Bell, unknown. (Getty Images. Photo by London Express/Getty Images)

The finalists in the Hospitals Cup on 8 May 1939. War would end the professional careers of some of these players. (Len Fletcher, personal collection)

Ipswich town centre was extensively bombed during the Second World War. This house in Myrtle Road was destroyed in an air raid on 2 June 1943. (David Kindred)

Right: The programme for a wartime match between Eastern Command and a Football League side. (Colin Kreidewolf, personal collection)

Below: WAGS of 1954: celebrating winning the Third Division (South) shield with at the Town Hall. (Len Fletcher, personal collection)

PROGRAMME

FOOTBALL 2530

In aid of EASTERN COMMAND ARMY WELFARE FUND.

Eastern Command *v.* Football League

Portman Rd. Ground, Ipswich — Saturday, Feb. 13th.

EASTERN COMMAND.

Colours—RED.

L/Cpl. Williams, R.A.O.C.
(Grimsby Town)

Gnr. Walsh, R.A.
(Sunderland)

Corpl. Anderson, K.O.S.B.
(Brentford)

S.I. Savage (Captain) A.P.T.C.
(Liverpool)

S.I. Brolley, A.P.T.C.
(Millwall)

Gnr. Murphy, R.A.
(Middlesboro')

S.I. Birkett, A.P.T.C.
(Newcastle)

Sgt. Strauss, R.C.Signals
(Aberdeen)

Gnr. Thornton, R.A.
(Glasgow Rangers)

Rfn. Burdon, Rifle Bde.
(Wolves)

L/Bdr. Lewis. R.A.
(Arsenal)

Referee : J. HOPE   K.O., **3 p.m.**

Conley (Fulham)   Goulden (West Ham)   Revell (Charlton Ath.)   Hall (Spurs)   Hopkins (Brentford)

McLuckie (Ipswich T.)   Ridyard (Q.P.R.)   Shankly (Preston N.E.)

Dawes (C. Palace)   Hardwick (Middlesboro')

Woodley (Chelsea)

FOOTBALL LEAGUE.

Colours—WHITE.

The Ground kindly loaned by favour of the Commanding Officer, H.M.S. Bunting.

PRICE 2d. Keep your Programme. Lucky Number wins Football.

Printed by W. E. Calver, 3, Friars Street, Ipswich

A Portman Road crowd of 23,050 watched Town lose 2-4 to Fulham in September 1961. (David Kindred)

The Manor Ballroom, owned for many years by the Ipswich Town Supporters' Association. (Kingsley Fletcher)

Alf Ramsey celebrating taking Ipswich Town to the Division One championship in 1962. (David Kindred)

Above: Champions: the team that won the First Division championship on 28 April 1962. From left to right, back row: Compton, Baxter, Nelson, Bailey, Elsworthy, Carberry. Front row: Stephenson, Crawford, Phillips, Moran, Leadbetter. (David Kindred)

Below: Tommy Docherty's Chelsea came to Portman Road on 12 October 1963. The visitors won by three goals to one. (Andrew Barnard and Kingsley Fletcher)

Above: Ipswich goalkeeper Roy Bailey in action. (David Kindred)

Below: A typical Churchman's crowd in the late 1960s. (David Kindred)

Above: Sherrington Park, part of Broomhill Park, thought to be the location of the earliest matches played by Ipswich AFC. (Kingsley Fletcher)

Below: Jonty's of Ipswich, originally owned by ITFC player David Johnson, one of many businesses run in the town by former players. (Kingsley Fletcher)

The Ipswich
Town Supporter's
Club stand
at the Suffolk
Show in the late
1970s. (Kingsley
Fletcher, personal
collection)

Ray Crawford,
Len Fletcher
and Ted Phillips
at one of the
ITFC annual
reunions. (Len
Fletcher, personal
collection)

Bryan Hamilton
with Pat
Godbold. (Len
Fletcher, personal
collection)

The changing face of ITFC marketing: a badge and a sticker of George Burley. (Kingsley Fletcher)

The changing face of ITFC marketing: an ITFC meerkat and onesie both sold in the club shop in 2013. (Kingsley Fletcher)

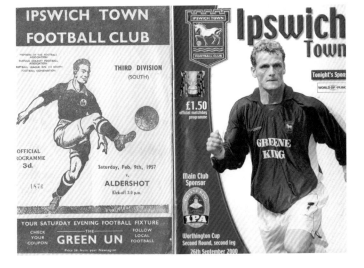

The changing face of ITFC marketing 3: Ipswich Town programmes from 1957 and 2000. (Kingsley Fletcher)

Above: A replica shirt with the Fison's logo from 1992. (Gavin Barber)

Left: A replica shirt, signed by defender, Manuel Thetis. Suffolk brewer's Greene King sponsored ITFC between 1995 and 2001. (Gavin Barber)

Above: Portman Road means as much to the young Town supporter as ever. (Gavin Barber)

Right: The statue of Sir Alf Ramsey has become a focal point for fans meeting up before matches. (Kingsley Fletcher)

Playford Road training ground and the location of the prestigious ITFC Academy. It was sold to Marcus Evans (Guernsey) Ltd in 2012. (Kingsley Fletcher)

Forza Town! The ITFC Italian Branch team (left to right): mascot Michael Ferrari, Simone Longo, Giacomo Grossoni, Claudio Longo, Luca Capellini, Fabio Cardillo Piccolino, Davide Casati, Daniele Longo, Frank Ferrari. (Simone Longo)

Youth: Town fan, Che Barber, who regularly travels to Portman Road from Oxfordshire, with youth academy products Tommy Smith (left) and Josh Carson. (Gavin Barber)

Above: Portman Road before the most recent changes: taken from the North Stand, the match was against Newcastle United on 11 April 1992. (David Jameson)

Right: Sir Bobby Robson's statue in Portman Road, decorated with supporters' tributes – including a Norwich City scarf – following his death in July 2009. (Joe Fairs)

Above: Police search supporters outside the North Stand before a match in 1992. (David Jameson)

Below: Enduring image: The face of Sir Bobby Robson on the North Stand now dominates Portman Road. (Kingsley Fletcher)

'Two years ago we gave the football club £42,000 in twelve months
... We have paid for everything on the football ground: the stands, the
offices and the dressing rooms ... We have never tried to dictate their
policy ... but ... tried to look after our own business. That is perhaps
where we have gone wrong ... Without warning, a notice appeared in
the press saying that they no longer recognised our Supporters' Club
and a new one had been formed ... We went to the Boardroom and
were given our notice – the secretary and myself after thirty-one years
and thirty-five years' service. We were not thanked ... we did not ask
for thanks and we certainly did not get them.'

However, this account of events does not mention that the split was initially
brought about by the resignation of ten members of the Association, who
would go on to found a new Supporters' Club. A more dramatic account
of the breakdown in the relationship between the Supporters' Association
and the football club is given in Ken Rice's club history, *Ipswich* (1973).
He describes how, on 13 May 1967, ten members of the Committee of the
Association handed in resignation letters to the chairman, Stanley Butler.
The members who resigned were led by the vice-chairman, Mr George
Knights, and a former vice-chairman, O. S. Nunn, very long-standing
members. Knights was a former player who had made a total of twelve
appearances for Town as a goalkeeper in the 1935/36 season and had
served on the committee of the Supporters' Association for many years.

The background to the split was connected with the setting up of
a fundraising body at the club that the Ipswich Town Supporters'
Association appears to have resented. For example, many fundraising
activities were taken over by the Development Association, run by a former
Town star, Tommy Parker. This included some of the things that raised
the most money, such as bingo. The Manor Social Club, which by this
time was a major concern in its own right – according to an advertisement
of that period, it had a Supper Room, a Grill and Coffee Bar and held
wedding receptions and other events – had caused division in the Ipswich
Town Supporters' Association because the upkeep of the building was
thought to be using up much of the money the association raised for the
football club.

The new Supporters' Club was formed, according to *The Men Who Made
the Town* (1986), 'in consultation and close co-operation with Ipswich
Town FC'. The book gives a concise description of what happened:

Differences of opinion between the Supporters' Association and
the football club ... came to a head when ten members of the ITSA
committee resigned and formed the Ipswich Town Football Club

Supporters ... Within two weeks the Football Club formally announced its recognition of the new organisation, recording its appreciation for the great assistance given by the ITSA in the past but adding that 'for the last two years the Board have been concerned about the financial support from the Association insomuch as monies raised by the Supporters' Association have not been forthcoming to the Football Club as could have been expected'.

John Jacobs, the Honorary Secretary of the Supporters' Association and a founder member, issued a statement expressing his surprise at the breakaway:

Every building on Portman Road was bought and paid for by Supporters' Association money. The trouble is we let ourselves be drained dry ... We put ourselves into debt over the new office building but we are paying that off at the rate of £400 a month.

After initially suggesting that the two groups should get together and 'sort themselves out', John Cobbold took action on 26 May when he announced that the club would recognise the breakaway group. The swiftness and decisiveness of his decision somewhat contradicts the traditional image of 'Mr John', the hands-off director who was happier delivering witticisms and drinking white wine than running the day-to-day business of the football club. His decision provoked an angry response from the existing committee, but they had in effect been presented with a *fait accompli* and at an extraordinary Emergency General Meeting in June 1967, all the members could do was decide that they would continue to exist, but that in future they would raise money for amateur sport in the area. Their relationship with Ipswich Town continued for long enough for it to pay off the debt on the new office building, however.

The president of the National Federation of Football Supporters' Clubs, Archie Gooch, was not impressed with Ipswich Town, however, commenting that 'there is not a better organised or more business-like group of people [i.e. the Supporters' Association] anywhere'.

From the beginning, then, it seems that the new Ipswich Town Football Supporters Club was in close co-operation with the football club and this has remained the case to this day. Over time, the new organisation developed other roles and activities, for instance, running the 'Blue Arrow' railway specials which took fans to away games, sometimes as many as 2,500. The current Supporters' Club has more than thirty affiliated branches all over the world, including in Australia, Italy, Hong Kong and Serbia, as well as a Disabled Supporters' Branch. It describes itself as a 'non-political' organisation that is 'a part of Ipswich Town Football Club, but ... run independently by volunteers ... [Its] main objective is to provide the vital link between the club and the fans, wherever they may be.' Activities and events include the annual Players' Awards and providing supporters with the opportunity to meet players and club staff at social events.

Ipswich Town Independent Supporters' Trust Club

For many supporters, Ipswich Town Independent Supporters' Trust Club is an important link between them and the football club, but as football has become a multi-million-pound business and clubs have become more remote from their supporters, there has been a growing movement to increase democracy and the participation of fans in the running of their clubs, typified by the Supporters' Trust movement.

At Ipswich Town, the idea of a Supporters' Trust arose after the football club announced that it had gone into administration in February 2003. The news was shocking for many supporters, who had been reassured by chairman, David Sheepshanks, shortly before that the club's finances were sound. Relegation from the Premier League and some poor decisions in the transfer market had led to a financial crisis, and many fans began to question the competence of the chairman and the board of directors.

In May 2003, the club's administrators Deloitte and Touche had proposed that Town entered a Company Voluntary Arrangement (CVA), which would make it possible for the club to come out of administration very quickly, possibly as early as May 2003. This proposal was accepted by the majority of those to whom the club owed money, although some of Town's unsecured creditors had little alternative and would lose financially. This included the St John's Ambulance Brigade, as well as some small local businesses, and saw a change in attitude from some supporters and local people who had until then been trusting of the people who had run Ipswich Town – perhaps to the point of deference.

Ipswich Town Independent Supporters' Trust, also known as Ipswich Town 1st, was launched at the Novotel in Ipswich in July 2003. It received the backing of some high profile former Ipswich Town players, such as Kevin Beattie and Roger Osborne, who attended the first meeting. The Ipswich Town fanzine, *Those Were the Days,* reported that the Supporters' Trust also had the backing of other former players, Jason Cundy, Russell Osman John Scales, James Scowcroft, Laurie Sivell and John Wark.

The Trust's stated aims were 'to unite and empower supporters ... [and] to gain supporter-elected representation on the board of Ipswich Town.' It planned to buy shares in the club as a share issue was scheduled for later the same year. However, there were problems even before the inaugural meeting, when the Trust's vice-chair, Peter Morris, stepped down after only a few week's involvement. According to Carl Day, the Trust's acting chairman, who is still involved with the Trust, Morris had realised that there were fundamental differences between the plans he had and the aims and direction of the other Trust members.

Morris, a South African, who had been living in Shotley and become a Town supporter, was the Head of Global Operations for Commerce Bank in the City of London. He had stated that he wanted to replace David Sheepshanks as chairman. 'I am not happy with many of Mr Sheepshanks' explanations as to why the club had to go into administration,' he told *Those Were the Days*. 'One day he is telling us Ipswich is a model of how a club should be run, the next it is in administration.'

With the club's decision to refinance through a share issue and a debenture scheme where supporters could buy their seats for ten or twenty years, the Trust saw an opportunity to give fans a genuine stake in the running of their club. It introduced a share scheme to enable fans that couldn't afford the minimum of £200 required by the share issue to participate in ownership. At this stage the club, under Chief Executive Derek Bowden, appeared to welcome the involvement of the Supporters' Trust and, according to the group's own website, the Trust had a 'great working relationship' with David Sheepshanks. But relations deteriorated when the Trust proposed, at the club's Annual General Meeting in 2004, that there should be a representative on the Ipswich Town Football Club board who was elected by the supporters. Following the arrival in 2007 of Marcus Evans as majority shareholder and the replacement of Derek Bowden with Simon Clegg, a former Chief Executive of the London 2012 Olympic bid, the aspirations of the Trust to be 'the conscience of the club' took a blow, as Clegg made it clear that he only wanted to deal with the Official Supporters' Club.

9

Jackie Milburn and Bill McGarry

When Alf Ramsey was offered the England manager's job in October 1962, following the retirement of Walter Winterbottom, who had managed the national side since 1946, it took him some time to decide what to do but, one month later, he decided to accept the post. Jackie Milburn, who had been an extremely popular centre-forward for Newcastle United and was at that time the player-manager at Yiewsley (now Hillingdon Football Club), rang Alf and asked if he had a chance of the job. Ramsey encouraged him to try for the position and Milburn was selected from over sixty applicants, which suggests that the post was not the poisoned chalice that some writers have subsequently indicated.

In his hostile biography of Ramsey, Max Marquis described the team that had won the First Division championship only one season earlier as 'willing, but basically inadequate' and was of the opinion that 'Ipswich's playing resources were slender to the point of emaciation.' He suggested that Ramsey was deliberately unhelpful to his successor, but the evidence is only anecdotal. In fact, the two men worked together until May 1963, when the outgoing manager took up his new role at Lancaster Gate.

Unfortunately for Milburn, he had inherited an ageing squad and he was unable to turn things around quickly enough, despite being the first manager to have a formal youth policy. Perhaps his biggest error was to sell his top goalscorer, Ray Crawford, to Wolves for a transfer fee of £45,000 which, to put the fee into perspective, was far less than the then record of £115,000 that Manchester United had paid Torino to bring Denis Law to Old Trafford in 1962.

Selling Crawford was a mistake in footballing terms; in the previous season he had scored forty goals in fifty-five matches. Of course, it was also a mistake because it immediately meant that Ipswich Town supporters felt understandably aggrieved at losing one of their favourites. Matters were not helped when Crawford's strike partner, Ted Phillips, left to join Leyton Orient, although he had not been scoring as many goals as he had done in the past. It is quite difficult to understand the thinking behind the decision. It appears that the motive was to raise funds to buy a wider range of players, which were certainly needed, but it backfired badly. Crawford would return to Ipswich in 1966.

The players that Milburn brought in, John Colrain from Clyde, Joe Davin from Hibernian and Danny Hegan from Sunderland, did not on the whole produce the goods, at least at first. Town finished the 1963/64 campaign at the bottom of the table and were relegated back to the Second Division.

Milburn has invariably been described as a 'very nice man'. John Cobbold said that 'perhaps his niceness was his weakness', but this begs the question as to why Milburn, who had no managerial experience at Football League level, was appointed – but then the same could have been said of Ramsey when he arrived at the club. It appears that Milburn's public image as a star footballer that was adored by supporters in his native North East, may have influenced the decision. It would not be the last time that Ipswich Town would make such an error when selecting a manager.

Milburn found the situation too stressful and his health began to suffer. In a biography, his son Jack Milburn, a schoolboy at the time, recalled that his father would 'splash out on a bottle and sit alone at the club or in a hotel room when away scouting and sip until he'd blotted the parts of his mind he'd intended'. After he left, Milburn claimed that he had tried to sign many players but was unable to complete the deals. However, he doesn't appear to have explained why he could not: 'In eighteen months I covered nearly 40,000 miles by car and many more by plane and train in order to try and strengthen the side.'

It was a sad state of affairs, and Milburn resigned in September 1964. Trainer Jimmy Forsyth took over as caretaker, assisted by trainer Charlie Cowie and coach Ken Malcolm, until a new manager could be appointed.

Bill McGarry was an altogether different character to Jackie Milburn. Pat Godbold remembers that he 'shouted at the staff and expected a lot of them'. He would 'kick the door and shout', but 'by the time he left he had mellowed'. Tony Garnett, the author of several books about the club, wrote that McGarry 'arrived in October 1964 to crack the whip and rule by a certain amount of fear'. Pat Godbold was then a young secretary and had been given presents by Jackie Milburn and Mrs Scott Duncan. 'Alf never bought me anything,' she recalls. Neither did McGarry, who she describes as 'tight'.

McGarry, originally from Stoke-on-Trent, had played for Port Vale, Huddersfield Town and Bournemouth and, in contrast to his predecessor, had a fairly undistinguished career as a player. He arrived with a reputation of being a tough, but effective, manager and he had been earning £3,000 a year at Watford, then in the Third Division. He was eager to move to Ipswich, and had some difficulty persuading the board at Vicarage Road to allow him to leave.

McGarry started as manager on 5 October 1964 and, in a phrase that would be unconsciously echoed by Mick McCarthy on his appointment forty-eight years later said, 'I am not a magician, neither do I perform black magic.' However, there were already signs of an upturn in the club's fortunes on the football field when, two days before McGarry's arrival, they beat the League leaders Newcastle United 3-1 at Portman Road.

In another comparison with the arrival of McCarthy in 2012, Bill McGarry's impact upon Ipswich's results was immediate. His disciplinarian approach seems to have had the desired effect. In addition, some of the unrest among the players appears to have subsided. Billy Baxter, never an easy player to deal with, had asked to be transferred at the same time as Milburn left, but the board had refused to accept his offer. Out of the twelve League games played in the 1964/65 season before McGarry arrived, Town lost seven and drew three. They were heading back to the third tier, but the transformation was so dramatic that Ipswich ended that season fifth, one place above Norwich. Only a month after the new man's arrival, Ipswich beat Portsmouth at Portman Road by seven goals to nil. Ironically, all the goals were scored by players who had been brought in by Jackie Milburn: Joe Broadfoot, Gerry Baker, Frank Brogan and Danny Hegan.

Bill McGarry was a single-minded manager, and he made a number of changes to the playing and coaching staff that were unsentimental but achieved the desired results. Roy Bailey, Jimmy Leadbetter. George Dougan, Larry Carberry, John Elsworthy and Bobby Blackwood all left the club, either because they retired or moved on to other clubs. Among the players who came in were a very young 'Mick' Mills and a South African, Colin Viljoen.

Mick Mills had initially come to Ipswich on a three-month trial from Portsmouth after the club had broken up its youth team. At sixteen, he had been too young to sign a professional contract, but did so just after his seventeenth birthday in February 1966. He would, of course, go on to have a glittering career as a player, captaining both the Ipswich Town side that won the FA Cup in 1978 and the UEFA Cup in 1981, and England. It was Alf Ramsey who gave him his first international cap and began what would be a distinguished career for his country.

Among the coaching staff, Charlie Cowie retired as trainer, having been at the club since 1936. He would maintain a connection by running a 'hostel' for young players. McGarry, like all football managers, wanted to bring in his own team on and off the pitch.

Sammy Chung would be his second in command and work as both a trainer and a coach. According to Pat Godbold, Chung was a 'yes-man' who would even cancel his own social arrangements if his boss decided he wanted him to spend the evening with him. He would also, allegedly, frequently 'lose' to McGarry at squash, despite being a much better player. Chung was born in Abingdon in Oxfordshire in 1932. His father was Chinese and he was only the second footballer of Chinese origin to play in the Football League after Frank Soo.

Reg Tyrrell was also brought in as chief scout. It was Tyrrell who had recommended bringing Mick Mills to the club. Between them, McGarry and his team would quickly bring success back to Portman Road.

Colin Viljoen was brought to the attention of McGarry by his friend Gordon Edleston, who was coaching at Johannesburg Rovers. Because of problems getting the young South African player a work permit, Viljoen started his Ipswich Town career as an amateur and was officially employed by John Cobbold as a gardener at Glemham Hall, which was of course a complete fiction. In the summer of 1967, Viljoen, who was only nineteen years old, returned to his native country; fearing that the player might not return to England, McGarry flew out to Johannesburg to offer him a professional contract. Viljoen would remain at Ipswich until 1978 when he went to Manchester City for a transfer fee of £100,000.

A final piece in the jigsaw that McGarry was putting together was the signing of John O'Rourke from Middlesborough, to replace Gerry Baker who moved to First Division club Coventry City in November 1967. McGarry had tried to sign O'Rourke several years before, but he was successful this time and the new forward scored twice on debut against Cardiff City at Portman Road. O'Rourke had been an England under-23 international and started his club career at Arsenal and Chelsea. His arrival at Ipswich in February 1968, for a transfer fee of £30,000, turned the season around. O'Rourke scored in almost every match that he played in, twelve goals in fifteen games. Town didn't lose another match after his arrival. Crawford was on scoring form too, scoring twenty-one goals in the season.

Ipswich Town were once again promoted to the First Division as champions on 11 May 1968 after a 1-1 draw with Blackburn Rovers in front of a crowd of 27,852. They had been undefeated at home for fifteen matches. Although it was only mentioned in *The Times* two days later in a list of teams that were promoted or relegated, underneath a report on the match between Newcastle United and Manchester City, which won the Championship for City, it was a momentous occasion for Town.

The Championship-winning team was: Ken Hancock (GK), Bobby Hunt, Derek Jefferson, Billy Houghton, Peter Morris, Eddie Spearritt, Danny Hegan, Ray Crawford, Bill Baxter, John O'Rourke, Colin Viljoen and Frank Brogan. 27,852 fans were there to see Town promoted and there was the inevitable good-natured pitch invasion at the end of the match.

Ipswich Town supporters must have been looking forward to the 1968/69 season with the usual mixture of nervousness and optimism, but they were in for a shock early in the campaign.

On 22 November, the *Times* football correspondent, Geoffrey Green, wrote a column about 'Changes at Fulham', but commented at the end about another managerial appointment: Bill McGarry was to go to Wolverhampton Wanderers. 'Wolves, like the Canadian Mounties, have at last got their man. They wanted McGarry four years ago when they summarily dismissed Mr Stanley Cullis.' Ipswich Town supporters who read the article may have also noted that the main story was the sacking of the Fulham manager, Bobby Robson, who would be temporarily replaced by player Johnny Haynes. The coincidence of the two events may also have been noted by the directors of Ipswich Town who, although they were deeply unhappy with McGarry's lack of loyalty, reluctantly agreed to release him. The club statement shows more than a hint of exasperation:

> The board decided to release him with disappointment and reluctance, bearing in mind that his contract was only signed a few months ago and the board went out of their way to meet demands.

Sammy Chung was named as the caretaker manager, but he would follow McGarry to Wolves very quickly, and one of the coaches, Cyril Lea, took over on a temporary basis. The favourite to get the job, Torquay United's Frank O'Farrell, turned it down. He would take a job at Leicester City in 1968 and eventually manage Manchester United.

Ipswich Town's star had risen to the extent that the club was being linked in the media with several big names: Bob Stokoe of Carlisle, Billy Bingham who was at Plymouth Argyle and the newly unemployed Bobby Robson, who came recommended by Chelsea manager, Dave Sexton, for whom he had worked as a scout. Billy Bingham was a definite candidate and was offered the job, but changed his mind at the last minute. In the end, it seems that there was only one man left in the frame and, in January 1969, the directors of Ipswich Town Football Club invited the thirty-four-year-old Robert Robson for an interview at the Great Western Hotel in London.

10

Away

Ipswich's first European tour was made to Bohemia, now the Czech Republic, which took place in May 1911. The trip was the result of contact made when a Bohemian international side had come to England in the previous year and played a match at Portman Road in front of 2,000 people. England won the game 10-1. The match was one of two internationals organised by the Amateur Football Association. In the other game, England played France and beat them 20-0.

Leaving from Harwich, and travelling via Antwerp and Dresden, the team played two matches against Slavia Prague, losing one and drawing the second. It must have been the first trip abroad for many of the Ipswich Town players. Players like Ernie Bugg, whose 'day job' was working as a plumber, would rarely have travelled so far afield at that time. The mini-tour was presumably a success, because in September 1913 another Ipswich Town team went to Bohemia. This time, Town lost all three of its matches.

Apart from some enforced overseas travel for some of its players during two world wars, Ipswich Town had to wait a long time until the next European game, and this time it was a competitive one. On 18 September 1962, Ramsey's side flew to Malta to play in the first leg of a European Cup preliminary round.

The Overseas Champion Club's Cup, always known as the European Cup, was a UEFA tournament that had begun in 1955. It has now become the Champions' League, but it was originally a knock-out competition and qualification was only for the national League champions of each nation. Having won the English First Division at the end of the 1961/62 season, Ipswich Town had qualified and had been drawn against the Maltese side, Floriana, who were part-time players on a wage of about £40 a year. Despite having Andy Nelson break his nose in the first leg, Town won 4-1.

During the game in Floriana, the Italian referee, Bruno Demarchi, awarded the home side a penalty, then rescinded it after he realised that his linesman was flagging for offside. The *Daily Mirror* reported that 'a typical Continental storm of jeers and whistles from the fans followed his decision'. The *Mirror*'s correspondent, Bill Holden, giving no credit to a team from a poor country that had been devastated by bombing only twenty years before, noted:

> Goodness knows what the tally will be at the end of the return leg ... This match – the whackiest European Cup-tie I've ever seen – began with Ipswich trotting round the track with their boots in their hands to the stadium's unfinished dressing rooms. At the end ten sweat-soaked Ipswich players, still in their kit, left by bus, for baths at their hotel and then a swim. And to round off the night, a couple of parties!

Holden was correct about the return leg at Portman Road, however. Town beat the Maltese visitors by ten goals to nil. Ray Crawford scored five, with Moran (2), Phillips (2) and Elsworthy doubling his tally between them. This scoreline remains Ipswich's best ever; but to put it in context, despite having one of the oldest and best clubs in Malta, the town of Floriana still only has a population of just over 2,000 people.

The Times report of the second leg was a little more realistic than the *Mirror*'s, although the writer seems a little unsure of which team to patronise the most:

> Ipswich, which found sudden glamour and excitement descend upon it as a result of winning the Football League championship last season, discovered only anticlimax ... The team's supporters packed the stands [indeed they did, attendance was 25,287], swaying with the play, 'oohing' and 'aahing' and waving their rattles. But there was really no excitement and precious little joy for them in this slaughter of the valiant but hopelessly outclassed team from Malta.

Ipswich Town had reached the European Cup proper and drew AC Milan at the San Siro in the first leg of the first round. Milan scored two goals in the first quarter of an hour. Ipswich was the side to be outclassed this time and only had two genuine chances, both of which were missed. Milan won 3-0 and left Ipswich with only a glimmer of hope for the return fixture. Despite winning the second-leg match at Portman Road, they went out of the tournament on an aggregate score of 4-2. Milan played a tactically astute defensive game, in front of a very noisy home crowd of 25,000, which was all they had to do with such a lead from the first leg. 'The lads played without luck,' Ramsey commented afterwards. 'We were the much better team. I knew it would be difficult to get back those three goals, but we deserved to.'

At the end of that season, Ipswich Town went on a short European tour with Jackie Milburn in charge, playing a short series of friendlies, Town lost against an East Berlin XI (2-1) and Kosice (4-2), but beat SC Empor Rostock (0-2), Jednota Trencin (1-5) and Spartak (1-3).

Ipswich would continue to go on such non-competitive tours, and would only again experience European football when Bobby Robson took over as manager and brought success back to the club. Indeed, their next trip abroad would be to face another giant of European football, Real Madrid, having qualified for the UEFA Cup by beating Norwich City in the Texaco Cup final the previous season.

Among the youth-team players that came through that season were Eric Gates, George Burley, Brian Talbot and Roger Osborne, and they were immediately involved in some of the highest-octane events that the club had ever experienced. Ipswich had narrowly won the first home leg by a single goal by Mick Mills. The *Mirror* reported that 'this lead is all they have to show from a match when the best of their attacking football floundered on the maturity and experience of skilled Real Madrid'.

Over 25,000 people had seen the first leg at Portman Road, but the away trip to the Estadio Santiago Bernabeu must have been an entirely different experience for the Ipswich players. The reported attendance figure for that match was 80,000. Whymark, Beattie and Co. were not apparently fazed by the prospect of playing in such an environment, or by the reputation of their opponents, 'Bobby Robson's men did not so much hold Madrid as outplay them for long spells, when the quality of their football threatened to totally expose and embarrass the strolling Spaniards,' the *Daily Mirror* reported. Unfortunately, five minutes before the final whistle, and presumably unimpressed that their side were about to be knocked out of the tournament by an obscure team like Ipswich Town, the crowd started to throw beer cans at the pitch and one struck the linesman. The final score was 0-0, but David Johnson had uncharacteristically wasted a fine chance of a goal just before the end of the match. Nevertheless, Town were through to the second round of a European competition.

The next team that Ipswich would be drawn against was the Roman side, Lazio. Once again, they were able to play the first leg at Portman Road on 24 October 1973. Town would go to Rome with a lead of four goals, all of them scored by Trevor Whymark. As Jim Lawton reported for the *Daily Express*:

If this was a night to savour the sharpness of Whymark, and the pace and trickery of Mick Lambert, it was above all a time to acknowledge the deep achievements of Ipswich chief Bobby Robson ... and to recognise why he is England's most sought-after young manager. Robson, in the last round, coolly out-thought the masters of Real Madrid. Last night his marvellously balanced team made the Italian League leaders seem like men facing football's Official Receiver.

Alf Ramsey, now England manager, was watching from among the crowd of 26,433.

The return leg at the Stadio Olimpico was a somewhat different matter. Norman Fox, in a low-key report in *The Times* thought that, following the 4-2 defeat which meant that Ipswich would go through on a 6-4 aggregate total, 'Ipswich Town could yet bring off one of the season's surprises by reaching the UEFA Cup final.' However, in the *Daily Mirror* Harry Miller reported that the match had been played in a 'white hot' atmosphere and that Ipswich would 'carry the scars and bruises of yet another outburst of Lazio brutality' when they flew home. It seems that as well as being an uncompromisingly tough side on the pitch, the Lazio players had also meted out some violence in the tunnel. *The Men Who Made The Town* describes events:

> When Ipswich were awarded a penalty in the 73rd minute it was the signal for the Italians to lose control completely. They attacked the Ipswich players, who showed commendable restraint in remaining cool and refusing to become involved, and Town supporters were also attacked and threatened by Lazio fans ... [The violence] ... continued right down the tunnel to the dressing rooms, in which the Ipswich team and officials locked themselves for fully two hours until riot police had cleared the stadium and they were able to leave the ground under police escort.

Lazio had, at this time, an unenviable reputation for thuggish behaviour, and the trouble had probably not come as much of a surprise. The atmosphere had been tense in the build-up to the game, and the disputed penalty decision proved to be the catalyst for violence from both the Lazio players and their supporters who invaded the pitch at the end of the game.

Bryan Hamilton told Dominic Bliss for The Inside Left football website in 2012, 'It was just physical and violent. They surrounded the referee, surrounded the linesmen and, to be fair, they did a great job of intimidating everybody. It was very much a rear guard action from us.'

Bliss also interviewed Lazio defender, Giorgio Chinaglia, who had lived in Wales as a child and played for Swansea City. He felt that the penalty given to Ipswich, when Lazio had felt that they had been denied one, had been the turning point. He and some other members of his team had attempted to placate their supporters:

> 'I was there because I tried to stop people going mad – there were fans smashing windows, throwing glass with their hands cut up; they were trying to get at the referee because of the decisions. The players were angry at the referee, at Ipswich ... at everybody.'

Asked if any of his team-mates had been among the masses banging on the Ipswich dressing room door, Chinaglia was a little less forthcoming. 'Perhaps,' he answered cheekily.

Trevor Whymark scored in the last minute, following his four goals at Portman Road against Lazio, in the third-round game, when Town were once again given a home tie in the first leg. An away win of two goals, by Peter Morris and Bryan Hamilton, to FC Twente's one meant that Ipswich had gone further than they had ever done in a European competition by far. They were in the quarterfinals of the UEFA Cup and would play Lokomotiv Leipzig in March 1974.

Ipswich dominated Leipzig in the first leg at Portman Road. 'Beattie was superb for Ipswich,' wrote Nigel Clarke in the *Daily Mirror*. 'He was the dominating figure in defence and the first to break forward in support of his attackers.' *The Times* was a little less complimentary. Its headline was 'Ipswich lose tactically but win the game', but it did point out an impressive statistic. Ipswich Town had not conceded a goal at home in the entire competition. They were to keep that record too, because in the away leg at Zentralstadion Leipzig in front of 50,000 people, Town lost 1-0 and Leipzig went through to the semi-final after extra time and a penalty shoot-out.

The turning point of the game appears to have been when captain Mick Mills had been sent off for the first time in his career for having retaliated when a Leipzig player, Löwe, had either punched Mills or stuck out his leg in order to trip him up. Either way, Mills had rashly retaliated right in front of the referee, who had brought out a red card. Mills had left the field in tears. After the game, he was described in the press as being 'inconsolable'. Robson said 'I don't need to criticise him. This man has gone through torture tonight on the touchline. I thought we were all heroes but we lost.' At the end of that season, Kevin Beattie was made the supporters' Player of the Year and was also awarded the Professional Footballers' Association Young Player of the Year trophy.

The following season, Ipswich were again drawn against FC Twente in the UEFA Cup, who this time put them out on the 'away goals' rule following two draws (2-2 at home and 1-1 away). Bryan Hamilton scored in both matches, but perhaps the most interesting aspect of the club's European experience in that and the previous season was the presence of a young Dutch player called Franz Thijssen. Although one *Times* report did list him among Twente's 'highly adept' players, he barely received the notice of any of the sports writers covering Town's UEFA Cup matches either in 1973 or 1974, but he was presumably noticed by Bobby Robson who would eventually sign him in 1979.

Ipswich's Town greatest achievement in Europe – and arguably the club's greatest achievement of all – came in the 1981 season when they won the UEFA Cup. Town had begun the season badly. In the League, they had been bottom after eight matches and were candidates for relegation for almost all the first half of the season, but they had ended that 1980/81 season at second place in the First Division and were FA Cup semi-finalists and winners of the UEFA Cup.

Bobby Robson said that Ipswich approached their European campaign 'one game at a time'. The first match was at Portman Road on 17 September 1980 against Greek side Aris Salonika. It was clearly a feisty, some said 'ugly', game. Three out of John Wark's four goals were penalties, and George Firos was sent off in the thirty-sixth minute. The final result was a 5-1 win for the home side, with the other Ipswich goal scored from open play by Paul Mariner. Town lost the away leg by three goals to one, in what has been described as a 'hostile atmosphere', Eric Gates being the only goalscorer for Ipswich, and went through to the second round to meet the Czech side that they had befriended all those years ago before the First World War, Bohemians of Prague.

Ipswich beat the Prague side 3-0 at Portman Road in the first leg. Wark scored twice and was then substituted by Kevin Beattie, who was only just returning to the first team side following a long period of problems with his knee. Beattie added the third goal in the eighty-fifth minute. Ipswich lost the away leg, which took place in freezing conditions. Despite this, the returning Kevin Beattie was feted in the English press. The *Daily Telegraph* said that 'Beattie was a giant at the heart of the Ipswich defence and his ability in the air was much needed to foil the constant flow of Czechoslovak attacks'. Robson, however, took pains to praise the rest of the team in his post-match interviews, adding of Beattie's return to form, 'I think he owes us that'.

In the third round, Ipswich came up against a Polish side, Widzew Lodz. They had knocked Manchester United and Juventus out in the previous rounds. Robson recalled that the Lodz coach had been somewhat over-confident, even attempting to have a bet with him about the outcome. 'They underestimated us,' he said. 'We knocked them out of sight.' Town won 5-0 at Portman Road in the first leg, including a John Wark hat-trick that took his European goals up to nine already.

The *Daily Mirror's* match report appears to back Robson's view up:

> [Lodz] were lucky to escape a bigger hiding – and even Ipswich, renowned for letting big leads slip away, should be safe with this commanding advantage ... Ipswich have really got the flavour for European competition this season on their own patch and they hammered away from the start to break down a Polish defence that never had less than eight men in it.

The only concern at the end of the tie was that the captain, Mills, was carried off on a stretcher with a badly gashed leg.

In the return fixture, Ipswich had to put up with even worse conditions than they had in Prague. Temperatures were at minus 14 degrees, and the *Telegraph* report described the match as a 'pantomime' and a 'farce'. Robson told the press that conditions were 'downright dangerous', but years later told an interviewer that the referee had offered to call the game off and he had refused, as the replay would have been in March and he was already thinking about how much his small squad would be stretched by that time. Nevertheless, he recalled that Ipswich were still dominant: 'We went out and smashed them to smithereens.' Ipswich won 0-1 and were through to the quarter finals.

They were rewarded by being drawn against St Etienne in March 1981. Unusually for Ipswich at that time, the first leg was an away match at the Stade Geoffroy-Guichard in front of 42,000 people. At that time, St Etienne were one of the most successful and popular European clubs. They are still one of the most successful clubs in French history, having won La Ligue ten times, and even had the honour of having a British indie band name themselves after them. Among their players in 1981 were Michel Platini and Dutch star, Johnny Rep.

Eric Gates had told Robson before the match, 'Boss, if we beat them, we don't have to play them in the final', and Robson felt that his side had what was required, 'Character and resilience ... it was one of the best English performances in Europe of all time.'

On a cut-up, muddy pitch, Ipswich won with four goals: two by Mariner and one each by Muhren and Wark. Rep scored a consolation goal for St Etienne. With an emphatic 3-0 victory at Portman Road the following week, Town went through to the semi-finals with an aggregate score of 7-2.

At this stage, Robson needed the calming influence of his experienced players and along with Mills and Butcher set out quite deliberately to keep the squad relaxed and confident. He was also concerned about the strain that success in three competitions (the League and the FA and UEFA Cups) was having on what was a small group of players, some of whom were young. The squad was tired and they had several key players out because of injuries. 'I knew there would be a mountain to climb,' he said later. After beating FC Cologne 1-0 at home, the second leg was going to be Town's third game in five days. Robson remembered, 'The players were feeling it – we didn't train. In fact, we went to an amusement park and it worked wonders.' Then the players 'knuckled down' just before the match, which they also won with a single goal.

The *Daily Mirror*, perhaps a little dramatically, reported:

> Ipswich last night showed the rich vein of character running through their ranks to march proudly into the final of the UEFA Cup. Their injury-ravaged, patched-up team put the sickening setbacks of recent weeks behind them to do a marvellous job in the second leg of the semi-final here in the Mungersdorfer stadium.

By the time Town faced AZ Alkmaar in the two-leg final, they knew that this was the only chance of a trophy that season. They had been knocked out of the FA Cup in the semi-final by Manchester City and had come second in the League. 'It gave us the psychological edge of having to win something,' said Robson. 'The players knew they were the best team in England. We had just lost the League, we were *so* unlucky in the FA Cup ... We just had to go for it.'

It is probably true to say that, by this stage, most of the country was behind Ipswich Town. *The Times* correspondent, Clive White, certainly appears to have been:

> They came into this momentous tie carrying the legacy of their 'successful' season – injuries to Mariner (Achilles tendon) and Thijssen (groin) and incalculable fatigue from sixty-four matches. It was no condition in which to be for the most important day of their lives. After seven seasons of the last eight in Europe, Ipswich still have nothing to show for years of cultured and often breathless entertainment.

The end was in sight as an exhausted Ipswich Town side beat AZ Alkmaar 3-0 at Portman Road in front of a crowd of 27,532. One fan, writing in the Ipswich fanzine *Those Were The Days* remembered:

> Portman Road was understandably buzzing the evening of the UEFA Cup final first leg, every other fan seemingly had a blue and white flag. I was in Churchman's and the noise was deafening (Churchman's sang

in those days) and the ground was packed. We played magnificently and won 3-0 in as good a performance as you could wish for in a cup final.

Over 7,000 travelling Ipswich fans watched the second leg of the final was held on 20 May 1981 at the Olimpisch Stadion in Amsterdam. Although they lost 4-2, goals by Thijssen and Wark ensured that they at last brought a European trophy home, although Donald Saunders, writing in the *Daily Telegraph*, sounded a little bit cross with them: 'They became far too complacent, allowed a certain slovenliness to mar their game and consequently allowed their opponents to take control.' *The Times* concluded:

> And so a journey that began for Ipswich in the heat of Salonika, and passed on through the frost of Prague and the ice of Lodz now drew to a close on a warm, sultry evening in the Dutch capital. Bobby Robson, the courted manager of Ipswich, must now decide whether he will journey on with them.

Once again, success for Ipswich Town supporters would be tinged with the knowledge that they would probably lose the man who had brought them such happiness, but they also knew that they would be able to take pride in losing him, as they had with Alf Ramsey, to the top job in English football.

In an interview for *The Boys of '81*, a film about that amazing season, Robson recalled his great side:

> We had a very good team ... A lot of individual technique ... within all the players and we found a system to suit every single player in the squad or in the team. Everyone in the squad had the character and the attitude ... They were a good unit, good integration between the players, great team work, everybody knew their job ... I built four different teams. The '81 team was the best side of the lot. It was the maturing of some of our home-spun players ... we bought well with Mariner and the Dutch boys were excellent buys, Muhren and Thijssen, and the development of Gates and Wark and Burley and Beattie ... We bought well in Hunter, our centre-half, Cooper, our goalkeeper was underestimated, very cheap... We bought well, never made a mistake and had this youth policy which paid dividends.

11

Bobby Robson

When Bobby Robson was sacked by Fulham in November 1969, he 'signed on the dole. I didn't know what else to do,' as he recalled later. This must have been a difficult experience for Robson, who came from a family of coal miners in County Durham. Robson's father had worked down a coal mine for fifty-one years and only missed one shift. His easy-going, twinkly persona belied a work ethic that lasted his entire life.

In 1986, Bobby Robson told Michael Parkinson, in an interview for the radio programme, *Desert Island Discs*, that he had always wanted to stay in football after finishing as a player, 'I knew what I wanted to do. I wanted to stay in the game. I was besotted by it, loved it very much and I think I had some – sort of – coaching qualities.'

That Robson was so very nearly overlooked for the manager's post at Portman Road has become part of his legend, as has the fact that he came close to being dismissed from his job almost as quickly as he had been at Fulham. He was hampered before he arrived because two of Town's best players were already on the transfer list. Danny Hegan went to West Bromwich Albion in May 1969 for a transfer fee of £60,000, and John O'Rourke was transferred to Coventry City the following November for £30,000.

Robson, in fact, made a good start at Ipswich Town when he took over the club in January 1969. His side won nine matches, drew six and lost only four. Given that Town were playing clubs like Manchester United, Everton, West Bromwich Albion and Wolves, it doesn't seem as if Robson did as badly at first as the legend suggests. Ipswich finished the season a respectable twelfth, which seems reasonable given that he had arrived half-way through the season after a difficult period in the club's history.

After drawing the first game of the 1969/70 campaign (against Nottingham Forest), Town went on to lose the next six games in a row.

Problems arose when the new manager began to lose the support of the Portman Road faithful, who would not have been aware that Robson was also having serious problems with discipline in the dressing room.

Robson's first season ended with Ipswich Town near to the foot of Division One in eighteenth place. By July 1969, he was forced to deal with open dissension within the ranks of his players. He was, according to Ken Rice, writing in 1973, 'obviously pretty tough but most pleasant, and his whole life is bound up with football.' He had worked as a miner himself when young, although he always knew that his ability as a footballer would take him away from that hard life, but he retained a strength of character throughout his life that was honed in that working-class upbringing in the North East. He once told his friend and coach Charlie Woods, 'Don't take my friendliness for a weakness.' Some of the Ipswich players at that time, particularly the 'old guard' who had been there for a long time, were probably even tougher. In retrospect, the intransigent behaviour of some of the players towards Robson probably explains some of the difficulties that Jackie Milburn had faced and perhaps even his inability to cope with the stress of managing Ipswich Town.

Robson brought in some of his own backroom staff, including Bobby Ferguson as chief scout, and made some changes among the players. The ageing Frank Brogan went to Halifax Town, and Bryan Hamilton was brought in from Northern Irish side Linfield. However, things did not go well on the field. Town seemed to have lost the ability to score goals and they lost to Norwich City at Carrow Road, which was always a setback for any Ipswich Town manager.

The tales of how close he came to dismissal in the early stages of his time at Portman Road are part of the Robson legend, along with his fights with some of the players. Many published accounts report that there were chants of 'Robson out!' at Portman Road, but one supporter who was there as a teenager doesn't recall any:

I don't remember anyone chanting 'Robson out!' I was in the North stand. I suppose it might have come from the West stand, but I certainly never heard it. We were too busy abusing the opposition. It may have occurred once, on one Tuesday night match. I wasn't there so I would have missed it. I think the hostility to Robson back then has been overstated though.

When Robson was chosen, I felt a certain amount of disappointment as, like most town fans, I had been expecting a higher profile appointment, notwithstanding the facts that McGarry had left because he considered Wolves a bigger club (which it was) and both O'Farrell and McGuinness, when approached, had stated that they didn't consider Town big enough for them (which it was). However, this was before the days of fans (and owners) expecting to win silverware every season and a football match, although important, was an event which, for the most part, you could decide to attend at the last moment, turn up at and pay at the turnstile. Some town fans still stick to this schedule!

Because expectations were not artificially inflamed, Robson's lack of success during his first few seasons didn't ring any alarm bells with me, at least, and not with other fans as far as I remember. All fans moan and the 'manager of the season' one week can quickly become 'that clueless dolt who'll get us relegated' the following. The Board, famously, are remembered for offering him a ten year contract despite, according to the press, Town supporters calling for his dismissal. I don't remember fans near me in the North Stand doing that and, bearing in mind that the managerial merry-go-round was a thing of the future (no panel of Sky summarisers waiting for 'Buggin's Turn'), I suspect that the Board's action wasn't much different from what their contemporaries at other clubs would have done in similar circumstances. After all, sacking the manager is a not only an expression of dissatisfaction with him but also a criticism of the people who appointed him and Boards of football clubs are not known for honest self-assessment. Also expectations were lower and 'fantasy football' had never been heard of.

The match in question was, in fact, on a Tuesday night, when Ipswich played Manchester United in the second round of the League Cup. A year before, the two sides had met and Town had won 4-0. The *Sunday Mirror* reported that George Best was 'just a spectator' as 'United came to Portman Road with their world-class stars and ended up humiliated. For once it was not Best, Charlton, Law and Stiles who stole the limelight. Instead Colin Viljoen, Colin Woods, Frank Clarke and Mick Mills led the honours brigade.'

A year later, on 7 September 1971, United had sent a slightly weaker team – no Law or Stiles, but they did have Best, Charlton and Kidd – to play in the cup game, and although Town played well in the first half, taking the lead in the eighth minute with a Jimmy Robertson goal, the referee gave the visitors a penalty to level things up. Town's defenders struggled with Best's skills in the second half and he scored two brilliant goals, according to match reports. The reporters in the Ipswich Town press room certainly heard chants of 'out'.

The next morning, Robson was called to the boardroom to meet the chairman, John Cobbold and, given the problems that both club and manager were having with the players at the time, Robson can hardly be blamed for expecting the worst. However, Cobbold only wanted to apologise to his manager for the abuse he had received and backed him to continue.

Robson's difficulties certainly did not end there, although having the backing of the club's board of directors may well have given him the confidence to take on some of the players who were definitely out to get him. It is quite normal for a new manager to arrive at a football club and have to impose his personality on a squad, particularly if the players are well established as they were in 1969 when Robson arrived at Portman Road. Billy Baxter had been at Ipswich since 1960 and was team captain when Robson arrived. It has been described as a 'personality clash', but Baxter was a very tough man who had been used to having his own way. He had already put in a transfer request when Milburn resigned as manager, telling the chairman: 'I don't see any future at Portman Road.'

Baxter was joined in his hostility to Robson by some of the other players, such as Tommy Carroll. Not all the problems were connected with the new manager. There was also some dissatisfaction among the players about their pay – a basic wage of £40 a week, plus incentives – that had led to the majority of the team ('eight or nine players' according to Ken Rice) threatening not to report for training. Most of the players did turn up, but Colin Viljoen, Steve Stacey and Tommy Carroll did not, although the matter was apparently resolved within a few days. Carroll had been suspended for what was officially described as 'a minor incident' earlier in the season and returned home to Dublin, but he had been reinstated. Several players, including Viljoen, had expressed the desire to leave and had been transfer listed. It was not a happy state of affairs and it was clearly imperative for Robson to stamp his authority on the dressing room if he were to stay.

In an obituary of Baxter in the *Independent* in July 2009, Alex Murphy wrote:

> Much of the nation's attention was focused on the team's free-scoring strikers, Ray Crawford and Ted Phillips. But Ramsey was well aware of the debt he owed the dependable Baxter, who anchored the middle of the field, defended staunchly, and won possession for Town's star strikers to shine. Although he was only 5ft 8in he was also renowned for his ability in the air, and scored a remarkable number of headed goals for a man of his stature.

Many players and Ipswich fans of that era would agree that there was no harder opponent than Bill Baxter. His toughness on the pitch won him the admiration of supporters. Off the pitch, it made him a difficult man to deal with. Events came to a crisis point when Baxter wrote a very critical article in a national newspaper in which he had claimed that Ipswich Town was 'going to the dogs'.

Baxter had been Ramsey's lieutenant and it was understandable that, now his career was coming to an end, he felt threatened by a new regime. Robson knew that Baxter was part of a clique of older players and he was in a power struggle with them. After a defeat to Leeds United, Baxter was dropped and he didn't like it. Robson recalled in his autobiography that the captain was 'another who had been making the dressing room an uncomfortable place, while testing me to the limits of my endurance. We lost the game 4-2 and they revelled in our misery, laughing and joking and ordering a bottle of champagne to celebrate the defeat.'

Even today, that kind of behaviour among professional footballers would be considered shocking. The culmination of events in February 1971 – a fight between Robson and Tommy Carroll, who was backed up by Baxter – resulted from an incident when Robson had pinned up a notice banning players who were not in the team on a particular day (and their wives) from the player's lounge. In retrospect, it seems like an obvious attempt by Robson to bring the situation to a head and it worked, although perhaps in a more physical manner than he had anticipated. Carroll had stormed into the dressing room and torn the notice down. It ended with Carroll and the manager rolling on the floor, and in Baxter's own words, 'Tommy was laying into him. Robson was shouting "Get the police..."' Robson's assistant, Cyril Lea, had tried to break up the fight only to have Baxter intervene, '[I] pinned him up against the door. When the dust had settled, Tommy and I went off to the pub for a drink.'

The two players may have felt it was a victory, but it was a Pyrrhic one. Robson immediately announced that both Baxter and Carroll would be suspended for ten days for 'a breach of club discipline and the benefit of team spirit'. They would both be transferred out of the club at the earliest opportunity. Writer Tony Garnett later made an interesting comparison between these events and what took place between two future Ipswich Town Football Club managers, Roy Keane and Mick McCarthy, when they were respectively player and manager of the Irish national side, in Saipan in the 2002 World Cup finals. Most accounts of this period in Ipswich Town's history are sympathetic to Baxter, particularly because he and Carroll were both sold – Carroll to Birmingham for a transfer fee of £20,000 and Baxter to Hull City for £12,000 – but it is difficult to see what alternative course Robson could have taken. The situation on and off the pitch was so serious that it could have only ended with Robson being sacked and, after his experience at Fulham, it might well have meant the end of his fledgling career as a manager.

In the end, the remaining players released a statement to the press backing the manager. Mick Mills, still only twenty-one years old, but now the captain of Ipswich Town, wrote, 'in view of recent events the senior players of Ipswich wish to make it clear that they are 100 per cent behind the club in the action taken against the management' and forward Frank Clarke added that 'we felt that by issuing this statement we could make it clear exactly how we stood. We players have been subjected to a lot of criticism recently and we just hope that this statement will clear the air.' It was unequivocal backing for Robson, who told the press, 'This is most gratifying. I appreciate this magnificent gesture on the part of the players. Perhaps now we can be allowed to get on with our jobs of playing football as well as we know how.'

Remembering the events with hindsight in 1986, Robson told Michael Parkinson:

> That wasn't too much of a pedigree to some of the players, so I knew it was going to be a tough time ... You need two or three years to get the dressing room and the player content right within your club ... There was a bit of a disruptive element within the dressing room at the club at the time with some of the players some of the senior players and literally they had to be removed. It was simply a case of getting them out before they got you out and the quicker the better and the tout-er the suit-er.

He was unrepentant about the fight with Baxter and Carroll and considered that it was something that 'had to be done' because they were undermining the younger players and the team spirit.

The atmosphere appears to have improved after the departure of Carroll and Baxter, as did the results on the football pitch. Ipswich ended the season in thirteenth place. Tough defender Allan Hunter came in from Blackburn Rovers and Ron Belfitt, a striker, was bought from Leeds United. Belfitt's stay at Ipswich would, however, be short. In October 1972 he left for Everton in a deal that brought a talented striker, David Johnson, then twenty-one years old, to the club for a transfer fee of £100,000. In addition, a happier Colin Viljoen withdrew his request for a transfer, and there were young players coming through the ranks like Trevor Whymark and Mick Lambert. Among other players that arrived at the club during this period was fifteen-year-old Kevin Beattie.

Robson's first trophy as a manager was the Texaco Cup, which Ipswich Town won in 1973 beating Norwich City 4-2 in the final over two legs. The Texaco Cup had been a tripartite competition involving English, Irish and Scottish teams, but the Irish had withdrawn because of the political situation in Northern Ireland, so that in the 1972/73 season, the following teams played: Coventry City, Crystal Palace, Ipswich Town, Leicester City, Newcastle United, Norwich City, Sheffield United, West Bromwich Albion, Wolverhampton Wanderers Ayr, Dundee, Dundee United, Hearts,

Kilmarnock, Motherwell and St Johnstone. Although the Texaco Cup was never highly regarded as a trophy, it was the start of a period where Ipswich Town began to be noticed as a promising young side and, most importantly, gave them an entre into European football competitions. In the same season, the youth team, which included Eric Gates and George Burley, won the first of the club's three FA Youth Cup trophies.

The developing side also finished fourth in Division One. Robson had quickly put his own stamp on the side and, with a chairman and board of directors who were more than happy to leave the manager to manage, he was able to bring young, talented players into the squad. It soon became clear that Robson had attributes as a manager that would work wonders for the club. Kevin Beattie recalled that 'his man-management to me was his secret to success. It didn't matter if you were the best player in the team or the worst player, he treated you the same and got the best out of you. He could make an average player into a good player and a good player into a great player.'

A team that featured regulars like David Johnson, Mick Mills, Kevin Beattie, Trevor Whymark, Bryan Hamilton, Clive Woods and Brian Talbot began to form the nucleus of the first of Robson's great sides and they ended the 1973/74 season in fourth place, qualifying for the next season's UEFA Cup. They would go out in the second round, but reached the semi-final of the FA Cup in 1975, losing to West Ham in the second leg at Stamford Bridge. It appears that they were unlucky to lose as the match report in the *Times* described Ipswich as 'indisputably the most skilful team left in the FA Cup', having all the possession 'for all but the isolated moments when Alan Taylor scored both of West Ham's goals'.

In that season, on 23 November 1977, Portman Road would play host to a Barcelona side in the first leg of their third-round UEFA Cup match. 33,663 people watched Ipswich Town beat the Catalan side by three goals to nil. Robson said that he had been 'very much afraid' of Barcelona before the match, which wasn't surprising given that one of the greatest football players of all time, Johann Cruyff, was in the side. Cruyff, however, was becoming increasingly disenchanted with football – he would retire from international football the same year and the following year he left Barcelona to play for the Los Angeles Aztecs – and he did not play particularly well against Ipswich that night.

The match was reported by Norman Fox in the next day's *Times* (entitled 'Ipswich brush past Barcelona artists'), 'Barcelona's team of many international talents proved brittle at Portman Road last night, against the characteristically relentless running and sound aerial control of Ipswich Town.'

Gates scored after sixteen minutes, turning a ball that had been put in quickly from the left by Clive Woods into the net. Barcelona had only one direct shot on goal in the entire match, when Heredia hit it straight at the town goalkeeper, Paul Cooper. Ipswich scored their second goal from another Woods cross into the centre, which Mariner headed down for Trevor Whymark to bundle over the line. Both Kevin Beattie and Colin Viljoen had been out for a long time with injuries but Beattie started the game. Viljoen replaced Eric Gates as a seventy-fourth-minute substitution. According to the *Times* report, the 'appearance of Viljoen for the first time in twenty-five months added to the good spirits of the crowd'. Clive Woods again created the third goal with a well-timed cross. This time the goalscorer was Brian Talbot.

'This is beyond my wildest dreams,' said Robson afterwards. 'I am surprised by our result because I was so impressed when I watched Barcelona on Sunday. They did not play anything like that well, but ours was still an outstanding team performance.'

Sadly, as almost everyone predicted, Barcelona would go through following the away leg on 7 December 1977 at the Camp Nou, but only after Cruyff scored two of the three Barça goals, in extra time and penalties. Town would console themselves at the end of that season by beating Arsenal in the 1978 FA Cup final.

Ipswich's achievement in winning the FA Cup in the club's centenary year was a remarkable achievement in itself, but all the more so considering that Robson had a small, young squad who were also playing in the First Division and the UEFA Cup. They played sixty-nine matches in all competitions that year with twenty-five players, and it is not surprising that they only finished eighteenth place in the League. On the way to Wembley, Ipswich beat Cardiff City (0-2, both goals scored by Paul Mariner), Hartlepool (4-1), Bristol Rovers following a replay, Millwall, who Town defeated 6-1 (this time Mariner scored a hat-trick). Following the defeat of West Bromwich Albion in the semi-final at Highbury, Town were at last in a Wembley Cup final against Arsenal, who at that time had a team of star footballers including: Pat Jennings in goal, Pat Rice, David O'Leary, Liam Brady, Alan Sunderland (who would move to Ipswich in 1984), Malcolm MacDonald, Frank Stapleton and Alan Hudson.

Town were not the favourites to win the FA Cup, although that may have been the media's metropolitan bias, because of their poor League form and the fact that they were suffering from a number of player injuries – 'patched up' being one common description of the side in newspaper accounts of the final. Paul Mariner had hit the bar in the first half and John Wark twice in the second, and Town certainly grew in confidence in the second half and began to dominate the game. However, the ball was not put into the net, and many of the crowd watching must have feared that once again, Ipswich Town would not get what they deserved and go home empty handed.

The *Daily Telegraph* reported that 'Arsenal, the hot favourites, can consider themselves extremely fortunate that the scoreline did not reflect accurately the extent to which they were mastered in every quarter of the field.' Twenty-year-old David Geddis 'displayed the sort of self-belief of which many an older player would have been proud. His was an astonishingly mature performance,' the *Telegraph* went on, and the *Daily Mirror* added that he had 'helped to run the Arsenal defence ragged'.

It was a one-sided match that defied the predictions of most sports journalists. Despite referring to the FA Cup winners as 'country cousins', *The Times* had to admit on the following Monday that 'their team outplayed, outran and outwitted mighty Arsenal in a triumph for the good things that football these days tends to forget'.

The single goal, scored by an almost exhausted Roger Osborne – controversially picked ahead of Colin Viljoen to play in the final – in the seventy-seventh minute did not reflect the game but it was enough for Ipswich Town to win the FA Cup for the first and, so far, the only time. Osborne had collapsed after scoring and was replaced by Mick Lambert for the rest of the match. A local youth team product, Osborne was one of a family of twelve from the Suffolk village of Otley. The Osbornes hired a minibus to take them to Wembley to watch the final. 'I walloped it in with my left foot would you believe?' Osborne told the press afterwards. 'The goalie had no chance. My dad will be pleased. He was watching only his second match.' Kevin Beattie's post-match comment may be the most revealing about Ipswich Town's dominance: 'I had nothing to do,' he said. 'It was as one-sided as that.'

Robson's comments to the press are typical in that they are all about the team, rather than individual performances. They reveal his pride in his team but that he also felt he had a point to prove – that his side were deserved champions.

> We were full value today, even Arsenal might be pleased they were only beaten 1-0. Before the match it was said the Arsenal have the more skill, but on the day we showed they did not possess it. At half-time I told the team not to sit back and admire the good work but to go out there and make sure we won. All departments of the team functioned today ... Clive Woods was good and so was Paul Mariner, but it's hard to single anybody out. It was just a very, very good complete team performance.

The year 1979 saw another record crowd at Portman Road turn out for Bobby Robson's testimonial match, which featured an Ipswich Town Football Club side that included George Best playing in an Ipswich Town shirt against an England XI. The teams played in front of a crowd of 23,284 and the teams were as follows:

Ipswich Town Football Club: George Best, Paul Cooper, George Burley, Terry Butcher, Frans Thijssen, Russell Osman, Kevin Beattie, John Wark, Mick Mills, Paul Mariner, Alan Brazil, Arnold Muhren, Eric Gates, Allan Hunter.

England XI: Joe Corrigan, Phil Neal, Kenny Sansom, Glen Hoddle, Emlyn Hughes, Dave Watson, Steve Coppell, Ray Wilkins, Tony Currie, Trevor Brooking, Stuart Pearson, Kevin Reeves, David Johnson, Peter Barnes.

Despite having had a testimonial match, Robson was to remain manager for a few more years, and still had his greatest achievement at Ipswich Town ahead of him: the winning of the UEFA Cup in 1981. But before that, Ipswich Town Football Club was to have another great game at its home ground when they beat Manchester United 6-0 in front of a crowd of over 30,000 spectators on 1 March 1980.

One of the key factors in Robson's success at Ipswich Town was the arrival at the club of two very talented Dutch players, Arnold Muhren and Frans Thijssen. Muhren, who had played for Ajax between 1971 and 1974, was signed by Robson from FC Twente in 1978 for a transfer fee of £150,000. Thijssen came from the same club in the following season.

In April 1979, the *Times* had written that Robson was being courted by Barcelona and Sunderland and that he was 'depressed by the size of the crowds at Portman Road', but 'Mr Robson's biggest incentive to stay with Ipswich is the maturing talent of the reshaped side which has benefited so much from the arrival of Thijssen and Muhren, the Dutchmen, as much as from the precocious ability of youngsters such as Osman, Butcher and Brazil'.

Muhren had been reluctant to come to Ipswich, and despite the club making great efforts to persuade him, he had at first turned the offer down. He changed his mind, according to Robson because of 'the lengths we had gone to and the area that he was coming to'. Muhren had been brought in to be the playmaker. Robson was aware of his vision and ability to distribute the ball and that those skills were to transform what was a very good side into a superlative one. In April 1979, Muhren was presented with the supporters' Player of the Season award at Portman Road by the Argentina star, Osvaldo Ardiles. He would leave Ipswich for Manchester United at the beginning of the 1982/83 season on a free transfer. 'Ipswich played like a Dutch team,' Muhren says of his time at Portman Road, 'and proved it was possible to play that way and be successful.'

Frans Thijssen had been recommended to Robson by Muhren, who knew him from their days playing together at FC Twente. He also won the Player of the Year award in his first season with the club. Ipswich fans had never seen anything like his balance, ability to dribble the ball and tremendous skills before.

'I did not know much about the club when I moved to England,' Thijssen told Sean Graham for an interview with the football website, scotzine.com in 2011.

In the past I played twice against Ipswich Town for the UEFA Cup. Arnold left Twente for Ipswich in 1978 and he had a very good feeling about the club so that made my move a lot easier ... The balance of the team was very good and we had quality in every line. We played more football than most English teams and that suited my game as a technical player.

Like most of Robson's players, Thijssen remembers him as a father figure who had made the two young Dutch players feel at home at a time when it was unusual for foreign players to come to England: 'He was the boss but every player wanted to give something extra for him.' Thijssen also left the club on a free transfer, to Vancouver Whitecaps, returning for a brief and relatively unsuccessful spell at Nottingham Forest.

Of course, as *The Times* had predicted in 1979, Bobby Robson's fantastical achievements at Portman Road would only end with him being courted by clubs like Barcelona, and following the UEFA Cup triumph, Robson was approached by the Football Association and offered the job of coach of the England national team. Despite being told by John Cobbold that he had a job at Ipswich for life and a ten-year contract on the table, Robson decided to follow in the footsteps of his predecessor, Alf Ramsey, and accepted the job, succeeding Ron Greenwood on 7 July 1982.

When Sir Bobby Robson died, several publications were issued in which supporters wrote about their memories of the great man. It is noticeable that they are mostly more about the man and his character rather than about the great football that he had coached his Ipswich Town teams to produce. Many fans recall how he answered their letters in person ('Bobby had taken the time to write a letter back to me, a mere seven-year-old – on headed club notepaper!' wrote one supporter). Pat Godbold says that Robson always answered his correspondence personally, 'every single letter'. Having worked as Robson's secretary for his entire tenure at Portman Road, Pat, who has worked for Ipswich Town since 1954 and has been honoured by the club several times, including a fifty-year service award in 2004 and a merit award made in 2009 when Bobby Robson was also honoured, went on to be his personal assistant for many years. When I asked her who, of all the people she had worked for, was her favourite, she simply answered: 'It has to be Mr R. [her name for Bobby Robson].'

Bobby Robson, for all kinds of reasons, has received so many accolades and tributes both during his lifetime and upon his death (all deserved), that it is difficult to find one that quite sums up the man and his contribution to the history of Ipswich Town Football Club. This is the tribute that John Wark, another genuinely great footballer who Robson brought to Ipswich from his native Glasgow in 1975, made when he died in 2009:

He was a top manager, not only of Ipswich but wherever he went after he left Portman Road in 1982, but he was much more than a manager to me. I lost my father when I was only twenty-two and Mr Robson was always there when I needed him ... But it was his knowledge of the game, allied to his ability to bring out the best in his players, which set him apart from most of his contemporaries. He also loved to see youth team players come through the ranks. It made him extremely proud and when we met at his home this year he rhymed off the names of all the kids he turned into proper footballers. There are a lot of us who owe him a great deal.

12

Youth

The man who should probably be given the credit for starting an Ipswich Town youth policy was one of the club's least successful managers, Jackie Milburn. Pat Goldbold, secretary to many Town managers from Scott Duncan onwards, believes that Milburn was the first person to take a real interest in bringing through young players; 'Alf wasn't interested at all.'

This may be because of Ramsey's attitude towards players and coaching. He is on record as saying, 'I cannot make a player improve. That is really up to the player,' but when Ramsey arrived at Ipswich in 1955, recruitment was still affected by the aftermath of the Second World War and, in particular, conscription of all young men into national military service.

The apparent lack of interest may also have been because generally there was little interest in youth football in Britain at that time. The FA had made an attempt to organise some kind of youth football tournament in the 1930s, but it had come to nothing. Most teenagers played for school teams or in local competitions run by organisations such as the Boys' Brigade. That is not to say that youth team football was non-existent at Ipswich Town under Ramsey. An under-18 side was entered in to the FA Youth Cup from the 1960/61 season onwards. They were knocked out in the first round in that first year by a Chelsea youth side who beat Town 7-0. The following year the Ipswich under-18s reached the second round after beating Brentford, but were again put out of the competition by Chelsea, this time with a less humiliating 3-0 scoreline.

Jackie Milburn's interest may, in fact, have been simply a practical one. When he took over from Ramsey he inherited an ageing side. Even his reserves consisted mainly of former first-team players with only a small number of younger members. He quickly brought in some younger players and made it clear that he intended to start a youth policy at the club, saying that one of his aims was to produce an 'A' team with an average age of eighteen at the most. The policy began to be put into action with the adoption of the Ipswich Lads' Club as a sort of youth academy.

In 1964, Ipswich decided to join the Mercia Youth League. The youth team also played in the South East Counties League and Cup and the Southern Junior Floodlit Cup. They proved to be a successful side and, for example, in the 1966/67 season, were winners of the Mercia Youth League Championship, Mercia Youth League Cup, Southern Junior Floodlight Cup and runners-up in the South East Counties League. Among the names that stand out from that season alone are Geoff Hammond, from Sudbury, who went on to play for Manchester City and Charlton Athletic, Mick Lambert, Mick Mills, Colin Viljoen and Ipswich boy John Miller.

In the South Eastern Counties League Cup that season, Town beat Arsenal, but lost to a West Ham side that included Trevor Brooking and (the elder) Frank Lampard. The same team defeated Ipswich in the FA Youth Cup that year too.

During this period, the club owned seventeen houses in the town. Ramsey rented one, and Charlie Cowie and his wife were given a semi-detached house at No.44 Crofton Road, Ipswich, which they would use as a kind of hostel for five or six of the younger players at a time. Mick Mills was one of the lads who stayed there when he was brought to Ipswich from Portsmouth as a seventeen-year-old in 1966. Later, the club kept a list of regular landladies who looked after young players.

According to Pat Godbold, Bobby Robson, who was always keen to attract talented young players to Ipswich and, of course, succeeded in doing so many times, used to go and see the parents of the boys that he wanted and tell them that they should send their sons to Ipswich because there was nothing for them to do there. There were no distractions such as night clubs in Ipswich, he would tell them; their sons were much less likely to get into trouble than if they went to clubs in Manchester or London.

Nevertheless, Robson has the greatest reputation among all the Ipswich managers for looking after his young players. Kevin Beattie came down from Carlisle aged fifteen. He had been invited for a trial at Liverpool FC, but had arrived at Lime Street station and no one from the club was there to meet him, so he went back home. One of the Ipswich Town scouts told Robson about it and Beattie was asked down to Portman Road for a trial. Years later, he recalled:

> The boss met me at the station, put his arm around me and said 'Son, welcome to Ipswich Town.' He had this dress code that you had to wear a collar and tie. When I got off that train I had nothing. He always said that I had a hole in the back of my trousers, a pound in my pocket and

my boots sticking out of an old paper bag. He gave me a shirt and tie and I've still got them to this day.

George Burley, who made his debut for the club at the age of seventeen, has said that 'Bobby Robson brought me up as a person, not just as a player'. After Robson's death, he remembered his first game, 'I ... had the small task of trying to mark George Best when we played Manchester United at Old Trafford ... Bobby believed in doing the basics right, day after day, week after week, forming you into the player he felt could play for Ipswich.'

Although Robson was looked upon as a father figure by many of this generation of players, he treated them as he would a player of any age and, according to Russell Osman 'took the view that if you were good enough you were old enough ... Bobby wasn't afraid to put youngsters in if he felt it was right for the team. I made my debut at seventeen because of that. Bobby showed faith in me and that built up my confidence.'

Mick Mills also recalls that:

One of Bobby's main fortes was to know not only when a youth player was ready for the first team but to also show the necessary courage to give the youngster a number of games to enable him to adjust to his new surroundings. If it's true ... [that] Bobby did not actually start the Club's youth system, it is also accurate to point out that he took it to an entirely different level by recruiting players from prolific areas such as Scotland and the North East.

Jackie Milburn may have been responsible for the beginnings of Ipswich Town's youth policy, but it was developed and became a fundamental part of the club's successful spell under Bobby Robson. Winning the FA Youth Cup at the end of the 1972/73 season was a sign of the shape of things to come.

The FA Youth Cup

Following the Second World War, the Football Association thought that there was a need to boost football among young men, and organised what was then called the Youth Championship for County Associations. The matches did not attract large crowds, but outstanding young players were selected for Youth Internationals and thousands were given the chance to play in a national contest for the first time. In 1951 it was realised that a knockout competition for clubs would probably have a wider appeal. The FA Youth Challenge Cup (season 1952/53) was restricted to the youth teams of clubs, both professional and amateur, who were members of the Football Association.

Ipswich Town are one of a small number of clubs to have won the FA Youth Cup three times. A few, like Manchester United and Arsenal, have won it more frequently, but Ipswich has a remarkable record for a small town club, winning the trophy in 1973, 1975 and 2005.

1973

A youth team that featured George Burley, Eric Gates and John Peddelty was the first to achieve success in the competition. Burley from Cumnock in Ayrshire, not only achieved great things as a player with Robson, including as a member of the FA Cup winning side in 1978, but is also among Town's most successful managers, taking them up into the Premier League in May 2000.

Eric Gates was originally from County Durham like his manager, Robson. His brother, Bill, played for Middlesbrough and he had a trial for them before he came to Portman Road. Robson also had to fend off interest from Aston Villa and Wolverhampton Wanderers before bringing him into the youth side in the 1971/72 season. Despite his success at youth level, Gates returned to his native North East, claiming that he was working on the land potato picking in a protest against not being picked for the first team. Robson was unimpressed and gave him a suspension and a fine, a situation which was eventually resolved following the intervention of the players' union, the Professional Footballers' Association (PFA). He went on to make it into the first team and have a long and successful career for Ipswich, scoring ninety-six goals in a total of 345 appearances, and was a very popular player among supporters.

Another young recruit from Bobby Robson country (he was born near Bishop Auckland) was central defender, John Peddelty. He went on to make fifty first-team appearances before moving to Plymouth Argyle for £50,000 in 1976. After football, he returned to Suffolk where he was a policeman for many years.

Ipswich Town reached the final of the FA Youth Cup in 1973 by beating Southend United, Leyton Orient, Coventry City, Bolton Wanderers and Swindon Town. Eric Gates scored to put Town into the lead in the first leg of a two-part semi-final against Chelsea, which meant that despite being held to a 0-0 draw in the second leg, Ipswich went through to the final against Bristol City.

The FA Cup final was also in two legs, as it still is today. The first leg in 1973 was at Portman Road and attracted a crowd of 5,556 spectators. All the players' parents were put up in a local hotel at the clubs' expense. In what has been reported as a high quality game, Ipswich won 3-0, with two goals from Steve Vale and one by Robin Turner. In the second leg at Ashton Gate, John Peddelty scored in the eighth minute, effectively putting the trophy beyond Bristol, although they did equalise.

1975

Ipswich had lost to Spurs in the quarterfinals in the 1973/74 season, but two years later were able to win the trophy back again. John Wark, Keith Bertschin, Dale Roberts (who would become George Burley's right-hand man in his successful management spell at Portman Road), Russell Osman and David Geddis all scored goals for the youth team that season.

The road to the final this time saw Town beating Leyton Orient, Bristol City, Fulham, Arsenal and Huddersfield Town. In the final against West Ham on 21 April 1975, Ipswich's youths made a great start by winning 1-3 away at Upton Park. A 2-0 win, in front of over 16,000 spectators back home, made this an emphatic victory over a side that has always claimed to be the 'academy of football'.

2005

Ipswich Town had to wait thirty years for its next FA Youth Cup, but given the subsequent careers of some of players in the Southampton side that they defeated in the final – Leon Best, Nathan Dyer, future Town player David McGoldrick and a sixteen-year-old Theo Walcott (Gareth Bale was an unused substitute in the first leg) – it was an achievement.

Ipswich Town's manager at the time was Joe Royle, but the youth team was very much the product of work by academy coach Bryan Klug and his colleagues.

David McGoldrick put Southampton ahead in the first leg at St Mary's with a penalty, after Aidan Collins had clipped Walcott, but Cathal Lordan had scored two goals early in the second half to put Town ahead, only to concede a goal by Walcott.

More than 14,000 people watched the second leg at Portman Road, an impressive figure as the game was also televised. Southampton dominated what was a lovely game in the first half, but neither team scored. Despite both sides coming very close to scoring, Southampton were only prevented by a brilliant save by Shane Supple in the sixty-fourth minute, and in the ninetieth minute Daryl Knights almost scored for the home side. The match went to extra time.

Later, Bryan Klug would describe Supple's save as a key moment in the game: 'You will have to go a long way to see a better save than that in the Premier League, Spanish or Italian Leagues.'

In extra time, a very dramatic final was made even more so when the fifteen-year-old substitute, Ed Upson, only called in at the last minute because Owen Garvan was unable to play because of a virus, came on and scored in the 118th minute.

Like the Southampton youth side, Ipswich's champions looked very promising but unfortunately very few of them – for varying reasons – ever quite fulfilled that promise. Shane Supple was one of Ipswich Town's most exciting prospects and was already on the fringes of the first team. He would soon displace another young goalkeeper, Lewis Price, for the number one spot. However, the club decided to sign a series of more experienced goalkeepers: Neil Alexander, Stephen Bywater (loan) and former Ipswich Town keeper and hero of the 2000 play off final at Wembley, Richard Wright, who returned for another spell. Supple was sent out on loan to Falkirk along with Billy Clarke, and later to Oldham Athletic when Bartosz Białkowski was brought in. Białkowski's time at the club was unsuccessful and he returned to Southampton. Shortly after Roy Keane arrived at the club as the new manager in 2009, Supple decided to return to his native Ireland, where he has pursued a successful career in Gaelic football.

Owen Garvan missed the second leg of the FA Youth Cup final due to a virus, but had played a large part in getting that far in the competition. He had what was probably the most significant career with Town of all, making 163 appearances for the club and scoring thirteen goals. An obviously naturally gifted midfielder, Garvan had a slightly languid style that was not appreciated by all supporters. He was sold to Crystal Palace for what seems to be the exceptionally low price of £250,000.

Aidan Collins, made four appearances for Ipswich Town Football Club's first team before going out on loan to Wycombe Wanderers and Stockport County. He signed for his hometown club of Chelmsford City in 1997, but is thought to have retired due to injuries.

Michael Synnott was one of the most impressive players in the FA Youth Cup-winning side. One of a number of young players recruited from the Home Farm club in Ireland, he suffered several injuries that affected his career long term. Manager Jim Magilton told the *East Anglian Daily Times*, 'He is the sort of character we want at the club. He needs an injury free season where we could get him out on loan after a good pre-season. That would give us an opportunity to see him step up.' He returned to Ireland and has since played for Dundalk in July 2009, then and Dublin-based Bohemian FC.

James Krause played as a defender in the Youth Cup final and represented England at under-17 level. He signed a loan deal with Carlisle United in 2006 and was released by Ipswich in May 2007, having since played for Rushden & Diamonds, Crawley Town and Cambridge City. James is now studying Sport & Exercise Science at UCS Ipswich, and working as an Academy Performance Analyst intern at Ipswich Town Football Club.

Sammy Moore arrived at Ipswich Town in 2004 after being in the academies of Charlton Athletic and Chelsea. He made one first team appearance for Town in 2006, but moved eventually to AFC Wimbledon, where he was Player of the Season in 2011/12.

Chris Casement made eight senior appearances for Ipswich Town, but like many of our talented youth players he went on several loan deals to various clubs (Millwall, Hamilton Academical and Wycombe Wanderers) before moving to Dundee in 2009. He played for Linfield in his native Northern Ireland between 2010 and 2012, but has since moved to Portadown.

Cathal Lordan, who scored two goals in the first leg of the FA Youth Cup final in 2005, signed for Cork City in 2006. He then moved to Waterford United a year later, before a stint with Blarney United. He rejoined Cork City in 2010.

Billy Clarke was thought to be one of the most promising youth players of this time. He missed the FA Youth Cup final because he damaged his medial ligaments playing against Spurs' under-18s, but celebrated on crutches with the team that night and was very much part of the squad that reached the final. Clarke did quite well for Town at first and made forty-nine first-team appearances, scoring three goals, but on the arrival of fellow Corkman Roy Keane as manager, things took a downturn. Amongst hints that there were attitude problems, Clarke left for Ian Holloway's Blackpool. Further injury problems have blighted his career, and in January 2012 he signed for the ambitious Crawley Town for an undisclosed fee. He scored for Crawley on 28 August in their League Cup second round match against Bolton.

Darryl Knights, although perhaps not always his own best friend, is both an Ipswich boy and a naturally talented striker. He made his first-team debut at sixteen but failed to play at that level again and, after impressing on loan, joined Yeovil Town in 2007. He has since played at Kidderminster Harriers and Newport County, where he won many admirers but, possibly as a victim of the latter club's managerial changes, is currently without a club. He was last heard of having a trial at Telford.

Liam Craig, a youth player at Town between 2002 and 2006, was the captain of the FA Youth Cup winning side. He joined Falkirk on loan after in 2006 and, after a loan spell, has had a successful career with St Johnstone, now in the Scottish Premier League.

Goalscorer Ed Upson was awarded a professional contract at the age of seventeen. He went on a series of loans and was released at the end of the 2009/10 season. He signed for Yeovil Town in 2010.

Danny Haynes had electrifying pace but lacked a clinical finish. Nevertheless he was in that group of players from this period who looked as if they would go on to have a successful career at Ipswich. Having played for Bristol City and Barnsley, he is now at Charlton Athletic.

Ipswich boy Liam Trotter was playing in the Felixstowe and District youth League when he was scouted for Ipswich. He signed a professional contract in August 2006 and went to Millwall on loan straight away. He had relatively few opportunities to show what he could do for Ipswich Town Football Club and after several more loan periods, he signed for Millwall in 2010 where he has been a popular member of the side, making seventy-three appearances and scoring fourteen goals.

Ipswich Town Youth Academy

It is certainly true that under chairman David Sheepshanks the club had a great commitment to its youth policy and it appeared to be paying dividends. Over the years, the academy has produced a number of players who have gone on to considerable footballing success and, incidentally, have earned a great deal for the club in transfer fees.

Richard Wright was a local academy product who was a very popular and highly regarded goalkeeper when George Burley was Ipswich Town manager. His prowess attracted the attention of Premier League clubs and for a time he was thought to be in line for the England national team. In fact, Wright was capped twice for England, but didn't impress and was not selected again. He did impress Arsène Wenger at Arsenal, though, and moved there from Ipswich in 2001, destined for what looked like a career at the very top level. Wright has played at many clubs, since including Everton and West Ham United. He has returned for short spells at Ipswich Town, but left again in 2012 and is now a goalkeeper at Manchester City.

Kieron Dyer was signed by George Burley as a seventeen-year-old and has been one of Ipswich Town's most talented and successful academy products, despite a career that did not reach the heights predicted for it because of illness and injury. Dyer asked for a transfer from Ipswich when the club failed to achieve promotion to the Premier League in 1999, having come close in successive seasons. He went to Newcastle United for a £6 million transfer fee in July 1999 and has since played for West Ham, Queens Park Rangers and Middlesborough.

Darren Bent came through the Ipswich Town youth academy and made his first team debut in 2001. He scored forty-eight goals and made 122 appearances in the League for Ipswich, but went to Charlton Athletic in 2005 for £2.5 million and has since played for Tottenham Hotspur, Sunderland and Aston Villa, commanding a higher transfer fee with every move. His latest, from Sunderland to Villa, was for £18 million.

More recently, academy products Jordan Rhodes and Connor Wickham, both of whom supporters had hoped would bring success to Ipswich Town, have moved on at an early age. Rhodes, whose father Andy had been a goalkeeping coach for the club, moved to Huddersfield Town for £850,000, much to the disappointment of many fans who had hoped to see him play for at least a season in the first team. A prolific goalscorer, he has since moved to Blackburn Rovers for £8 million. Wickham, who again was looked on as the great hope of an Ipswich revival, moved to Sunderland in June 2011 for a little over £8 million.

Other notable products of the Ipswich Town youth system have been Dalian Atkinson, Chris Kiwomya, James Scowcroft, Dean Bowditch and, more recently, Luke Hyam, Josh Carson and New Zealand international, Tommy Smith.

The Ipswich Town Youth Academy was set up in 1998 with youth team coach Bryan Klug as its head. He went to Tottenham Hotspur as head of player development in 2010, but returned to run the academy in 2012, a decision that was very popular with Ipswich Town supporters. The future of the Ipswich Town academy has been under scrutiny in recent years. Changes have been imposed on Football League clubs under a system called the Elite Player Performance Plan (EPPP), placing conditions on how academies are run and requiring clubs to apply to run their academies at different levels or 'categories'. There has been some controversy resulting from the club's decision to apply for Category Two status, but recent statements from Ipswich Town have suggested that they will be applying for Category One at a future date.

In a reply to a letter to an Ipswich Town supporter, written in about 1995, when Bobby Robson was manager at FC Porto, he wrote, 'What has gone wrong at Ipswich has been the youth policy – always the backbone of the club – and selective purchasing.' Robson was very proud of the very young players that he had brought through – Beattie, Butcher ('players he regarded almost as sons', according to writer David Huxley), Wark, Burley and Gates among them – and often referred to his strong belief that a good youth system was key to success.

It is not unreasonable to claim that, particularly since the time of Bobby Robson, youth team football and, more recently, a youth academy, have been a central part of Ipswich Town's identity as a football club. It has been something that many supporters hold dear, having seen very talented young players come through the youth system many times over. It may be that because such a youth policy has served the club so well for forty years or it may simply be that it is felt, viscerally, to be part of Sir Bobby Robson's legacy. Whatever the reason, a thriving youth academy has become part of what supporters regard as the club's identity.

13

Ferguson, Duncan, Lyall

The departure for England of a manager of Robson's stature was always going to be a problem for Ipswich Town. His replacement was an internal promotion, Bobby Ferguson, who had been a coach at Portman Road for eleven years. 'I suppose it's a bit like Bob Paisley taking over from Bill Shankly,' he said, optimistically.

Ferguson was from Newcastle upon Tyne like Robson, and had played as a full-back for Newcastle United, Derby County and Cardiff City between 1955 and 1968. He came to work at Portman Road as a coach and was the youth-team coach when Ipswich won the FA Youth Cups in 1973–75. It was a promising *curriculum vitae,* but Ferguson struggled with the administrative aspects of his job and was suspicious of the media, two things at which Robson had excelled. He may have benefited from some help in those areas, but Ipswich did not employ many administrative staff and the chairman, now Patrick Cobbold following the retirement of his brother John, maintained the family policy of letting the manager 'get on with it'. It had been a brilliant strategy with managers of the calibre of Ramsey and Robson at the helm, less so with ordinary mortals.

Despite inheriting a squad with players of the quality of Wark, Gates, Mariner, Thijssen, Brazil, Butcher, McCall, Burley and Osman, Ferguson's Ipswich Town began the 1982/83 season with six successive defeats in Division One and were beaten by AS Roma at the Stadio Olimpico in the first leg of the UEFA Cup first round. There was a brief revival when they beat Notts County 0-6 and they also won the second-leg match against Roma (but went out of the tournament on aggregate). Following another string of five games without a win, Town recovered somewhat and ended the season in ninth place.

In addition to this, many of the supporters' favourites were leaving, including Muhren who went to Manchester United, Frans Thijssen who moved to the Vancouver Whitecaps and, controversially, Mick Mills, who was sold to Southampton for £40,000. Many supporters believed that the cost of the new Pioneer stand was the reason for the departure of the players and this was particularly the case when Brazil, one of the club's younger stars, left for Tottenham Hotspur for £500,000.

He and Ferguson did not get on, and on at least one occasion Brazil had not followed the instructions that his manager had given him when he went on to the pitch. Brazil had not always been easy for Robson to manage, and the player had not enjoyed training in particular. On one occasion when Brazil, whom Robson nicknamed Pele, was not making any effort on the training pitch, Robson shouted over to Brazil, 'Pele, get a shower and go home.' Brazil ran off the field straight away, but as Pat Godbold recalled, 'He played a blinder on the Saturday.'

Ferguson could be forgiven for not having the man-management skills of a Robson, but his explanation of Brazil's departure to the media raised more questions than it answered:

> It was with a certain amount of reluctance that the club agreed to his request for transfer. I wondered at the time whether there was any point trying to keep a player who clearly saw his future elsewhere. I cannot conceal the fact, either, that the present financial position has a lot to do with the club accepting Tottenham's offer. The cash we received for Alan will go a long way towards easing the burden.

Further transfer requests came from John Wark and Paul Mariner, who wanted substantial pay rises. Ferguson took the captaincy away from Mariner in response, making first Russell Osman and then Terry Butcher his replacement. Mariner left in February 1984 for Arsenal. Despite some positive developments, like the arrival in the first team of schoolboy Jason Dozzell, it seems obvious that the atmosphere at Portman Road was not a good one. They finished the 1983/84 season mid-table.

Ferguson once again blamed financial problems at the club for the loss of Mariner, saying 'here at Portman Road, we are certainly feeling the pinch', but some supporters were angry that he and Wark were rumoured to have made demands for as much as £1,000 a week. Ferguson brought Alan Sunderland in from Arsenal to replace Mariner and, when Wark moved to Liverpool for £450,000, Romeo Zondervan from West Bromwich Albion, but as Ferguson himself admitted, 'Nothing could really compensate for the loss of John Wark.'

Falling attendances, because of the poor performances on the pitch, compounded the club's financial problems. Nevertheless, Ferguson was offered a contract for a further two years. By the end of the 1985/86 season, his fourth season in charge of the club, Ipswich Town had been relegated from the First Division. They had been in the top flight for seventeen years.

Ferguson's problems were not just about whether he was a good manager or not, or even that anyone who followed Bobby Robson into the job at Ipswich would have found it difficult to carry on at such a high level. Ferguson – and this is, of course, true for all his successors as Ipswich Town manager – also had to cope with the massive, rapid changes in the way that football was run which began at this time, and have been described as a 'football revolution'. The wage demands of some of Ferguson's players were the opening salvos in which players – and more notably, their agents – sought to strengthen their position in the power structure of the game. They became aware that it was they, or at least the Maradonas of this world, who were the ones attracting the television cameras (and therefore the great influx of money) to the game. Even the journeymen players saw it as an opportunity to take advantage and increase their living standards prodigiously.

There was a conscious attempt, in reports like the Football Association's *Blueprint for the Future of Football,* to restructure the game and widen its appeal. The arrival of global media corporations, such as Rupert Murdoch's Sky Television, meant that there was more money than ever available to football clubs. It was a revolution, and Ipswich, a club that had taken decades to evolve even into a professional club, could not ignore what was happening if it wanted to stay at the top of English football. It was no longer possible for a football club to survive with a manager who combined coaching with general administrative tasks like ordering toilet rolls and making sure the public areas had been cleaned, as Bobby Robson had done. Even lower League clubs began to appoint accountancy and media experts, merchandising managers and chief executives.

A mixed season the following year, 1986/87, saw Ipswich reach fifth place in the Second Division and narrowly miss out on an immediate return to the First, only losing to Charlton Athletic in the second leg of the play-off final. Ferguson didn't travel back to Ipswich with his team. Presumably he had either been told or worked out for himself that his time as the Ipswich Town manager was over. A few days later, the club announced that his contract would not be renewed, thus continuing the fiction that Ipswich Town Football Club had never sacked a manager. In fact, Ipswich's first manager Mick O'Brien had been dismissed, and the club had been lucky in that they had two managers who were so successful that they went straight from Portman Road to coach the England national team. It was true that the Cobbold family had been reluctant to remove their managers; however, although it could also be argued that in some cases delaying the removal of a manager like Ferguson may have been detrimental to the club long term, it is equally true to say that a great deal of Town's success under Ramsey and Robson was for the very reason that they were given enough time to build up a side and had been left to manage and not interfered with by the board of directors.

John Duncan was appointed as Bobby Ferguson's successor. Initially, Ipswich had approached Mick Mills, then managing Stoke City, but the club had been refused Ipswich permission to speak to its former captain. There had also been applications from several other people, including long-time coach, Charlie Woods. Duncan, who had been managing Chesterfield, retained Woods as his assistant while bringing in some of his own people with whom he replaced several long-serving members of the backroom staff.

Paul Cooper left on a free transfer before Duncan's arrival and Kevin Wilson went to Chelsea for a fee of £335,000 over the summer. Duncan brought in Graham Harbey, Neil Woods and David Lowe. It became obvious to supporters quite quickly that Duncan's team would not be playing the kind of passing football that they had grown accustomed to under Bobby Robson.

There were some popular new arrivals, including Dalian Atkinson, who was spotted playing in Shrewsbury by a scout and had five seasons with the club and Simon Milton, who had been playing for a Suffolk non-League side, Bury Town. He would play for Ipswich until 1998, but his association with the club would be even more long term as he has worked for the club in various roles ever since and is currently Player Liaison Officer.

John Duncan's side finished his first season in a respectable eighth place, but the supporters were neither used to the Second Division, nor happy with the type of football that they now had to watch. Paul Cooper was replaced in goal by Craig Forrest, a Canadian who had come through the Ipswich Town youth system, in goal. Other arrivals were David Linighan from Shrewsbury, for a then record fee of £300,000 and David Hill from Scunthorpe for £80,000. Players, like Mark Brennan, a talented youngster who had been brought into the Ipswich side by Bobby Ferguson, became unhappy with the new manager's style of play and tactics. Although Duncan went to some effort to dissuade Brennan from his intention of leaving – even, according to Tony Garnett, making sure he had Brennan's favourite brand of lager on hand for a heart-to-heart chat in his office – the player went to Middlesbrough in July 1988.

Duncan's second season in charge was similar to his first and Town finished in ninth place, one below the previous season, but there were some depressing results for supporters who had recent memories of European glory, including a 5-0 defeat at Port Vale, a Potteries club that had spent most of its life in the Fourth Division. It was the change in the way that the team played, however, which caused the greatest unhappiness for fans, and supporters' attitudes were also changing. Higher ticket prices and the massively raised profile of the game of football itself raised expectations. For the first time since it had become a professional club, Ipswich Town was faced with organised protests by its own fans, including in one instance, the burning of an effigy of John Duncan. It was only a matter of time before the manager would have to leave, and he was sacked at the end of the season.

John Lyall had lost his job as manager at West Ham after they had been relegated, so might have seemed an unlikely candidate to bring success back to Ipswich Town. He had a good reputation, however, and although he had not achieved the success that Robson did at Ipswich, Lyall had rebuilt his West Ham side several times and turned them into a side that had competed in the UEFA Cup and reached their highest ever League position when they finished the 1985/86 season in third place in the First Division. Lyall did not make any major backroom changes, but brought his assistant from Upton Park, Mick McGiven with him as first-team coach.

The *Daily Mirror* reported that Ipswich were about to appoint Lyall in its edition on 10 May 1990:

> John Lyall will be confirmed as the new manager of Ipswich within the next twenty-four hours ... Lyall has been working as technical advisor to Terry Venables at Tottenham Hotspur since getting the boot from West Ham last year ... There has been no shortage of demands on his services. But Lyall has resisted all overtures, claiming it would take something very special to lure him away from Spurs.
>
> The item also added that one of the attractions would be a record salary of around £65,000 a year.

Lyall had been upset by the manner of his dismissal from his former club and presumably felt that he had a point to prove. Town finished fourteenth in his first season at the club, but in a remarkable turnaround, Ipswich was promoted as champions and took their place in the very first season of the new Premier League as the top division in English football.

Lyall had achieved this minor miracle with a team that was mostly made up of talented but unproven young players, several of whom – like Craig Forrest, Simon Milton, Gavin Johnson, Micky Stockwell and Chris Kiwomya – were either local or had come through the Ipswich youth system. He made few signings and spent very little on 'names', but a few players, like Geraint Williams or Steve Whitton who had played for Lyall at West Ham, came in and John Wark returned to the club. In the view of one supporter from that time, Ipswich went back to playing 'proper football with proper footballers'. They had begun to play good quality, passing football again and it paid off.

Ipswich were promoted, after a six-year spell in the second division, at Oxford, where the home side were facing relegation. Although Ipswich were the better footballing side, Oxford had to fight hard and a future Town star, Jim Magilton, put them in front. Gavin Johnson headed an equaliser in soon afterwards and at the end of the match Ipswich Town supporters knew that they would be part of the inaugural Premier League.

Without going into an account of the history of the Premier League or an analysis of its effect upon football in England since 1992, it is fair to say that its foundation, which was the culmination of various attempts to form a breakaway elite League driven by television money, brought about the most profound changes. At the time, it was a great coup for Ipswich Town to be part of that elite, but the achievement brought pressures of its own, particularly financial ones.

Lyall brought in new players, including Bulgarian international, Bontcho Guentchev from Sporting Lisbon, who had been recommended by Bobby Robson, and Paul Mason from Aberdeen. Ian Marshall, a forward, came in, signed from Oldham Athletic for £100,000 where Joe Royle had been playing him as a defender. Ipswich finished their first season in the Premier League just above the relegation places, at sixteenth. The following season, they would have an even narrower escape, ending just above the drop zone in nineteenth place.

Although Lyall won Ipswich supporters over by bring back the style of football that they liked and giving opportunities to young players, there was a feeling that he was not completely committed to the club and that this would be his last managerial appointment before retiring. His less popular assistant, Mick McGiven, was in charge of the first team on a day-to-day basis and did all the coaching, Lyall having a more detached role. As Henderson and Voller wrote in their history of the club, 'He kept his distance, chose not to appear at many social events and rarely opened up in the press. He was a bit of a stranger to the fans, even after four years at the helm.'

In fact, following such a poor second season in the Premier League, Lyall appeared to be withdrawing more and more from the daily running of team affairs rather than taking back the leadership role. Mick McGiven became the club's 'football development officer' and former players John Wark and Paul Goddard took over the coaching role. More players were brought in like Steve Sedgley from Spurs and Town went looking further afield. Having sent chief scout Charlie Woods to South America, two new players arrived; Adrian Paz from Uruguay and Mauricio Taricco from Argentina.

Taricco in particular would become a fans' favourite, but the arrival of the new players in reality presaged what has often been described as the 'worst season in the club's history', which among other depressing things, saw Ipswich have a run of eight successive defeats, including conceding four goals in away matches at both Leeds and Highbury. In fact, Town only won two of its last fifteen games in the Premier League, and they inevitably ended the 1994/95 season in twenty-second place and were relegated to the second division, which was now calling itself the First Division. They finished at the very bottom of the League table and had only managed to collect twenty-seven points in the entire season.

The season also saw a change at the top of the club's administration with the appointment of David Sheepshanks, who had been on the board of directors since 1987, as chairman. Although he was an old Etonian, like John and Patrick Cobbold, David Sheepshanks was a break with the past in that he had no connection with that family. He was a Suffolk-based businessman, running Suffolk Foods with his brother. He was very much a man for the new football era, combining a genuine and profound love for Ipswich Town Football Club with a fondness for business language. There was much talk of 'Five Year Plans' and the development of the club at the top level. Sheepshanks also had strong connections with the Football Association – he was on the FA board for many years – and with the directors of other clubs, like Rupert Lowe at Southampton and David Dein at Arsenal. His vision for the club, combined with his undoubted ambition, sat well with the supporters for many years. David Sheepshanks would always place much importance on what were regarded as the Ipswich Town traditions and values – 'the Ipswich Way', a concept that may well have been overstated in the past but is still held dear by many fans. Very much the 'modern' football chairman, Sheepshanks would oversee a period of both great joy and pain for the Ipswich Town faithful.

14

Identity & Image

Tradition is an important part of being a football supporter, and for better or worse, Ipswich Town fans have arguably been more attached to their past than most. That is partly because of the club's serendipity in finding two of the greatest managers in Alf Ramsey and Bobby Robson, who brought unheralded success and turned Ipswich from an obscure small town team to a household name, celebrated not only for the style and quality of its football around the world, but also for the example set by the board of directors in allowing both men the time and space to build their teams in the way that they wanted to.

There are many football clubs in towns of a similar size to Ipswich that have never had remotely comparable experiences, such as becoming First Division champions or winning a major European trophy. But for those glory years, Ipswich Town might well have had a similar fate to the Shrewsburys or Swindons of the lower leagues.

In the time since the Premier League was founded in 1992, the club's fortunes have changed dramatically – two spells in the top division and some further European adventures on the one hand, massive financial problems on the other. In this, Ipswich Town is no longer untypical. It is the same for many clubs, Coventry City and Portsmouth being examples of how things can go awry. The vast sums of money involved in the game, mainly coming through satellite television, have attracted investors that have little or no interest in football. Marketing, merchandising and media posts have as much importance at the modern football club as coaches and physiotherapists do. Some clubs even employ 'brand protection managers' to ensure that the symbolic aspects of a club's traditions and history are retained as assets to be exploited by the club alone in order to bring in much-needed revenue. Supporters may regard things like the team's name, the colour and design of the kit, the name of the ground, the crest or badge as part of their identity as fans and members of their club, but these things are all now part of the image of a football club and as such, they are owned, copyrighted, trademarked and have a financial value.

Like all clubs, Ipswich Town has its own shop, Planet Blue, which along with the more traditional replica kits, hats and scarves now sells Ipswich Town branded plastic ducks, cuddly meerkats and onesies. With the constant pressure to increase revenue, the club must always find new ways of encouraging supporters to spend their money on Ipswich Town branded produce.

A good example of this is in the adoption of what are essentially fictional 'traditions'. Whereas in the past club nicknames and songs came from the terraces or evolved over time, in recent decades they appear to be invented or picked up by the club or the media in the form of competitions, or passing fads which are then seized upon and turned into marketing opportunities. The current club crest, featuring a white Suffolk punch, was the result of one such competition in 1972 won by John Gammage, then the treasurer of the Supporters' Club. Even so, his idea had been to draw upon local traditions:

> I regarded the Suffolk Punch as a noble animal, well suited to dominate our design and represent the club. And to complete the badge I thought of the town of Ipswich that contains many historical buildings, including the Wolsey Gate, and is close to the sea with a large dock area.

Since the use of the Suffolk Punch on the crest, the image of the heavy horse has been taken up and used as a club icon including the team's mascots, Bluey and Crazee. In some ways, it is a strange choice, relating far more to the farming traditions of the county of Suffolk than the port of Ipswich, but perhaps has reflected a growing trend for supporters who come from outside the town, although relatively few of them have any direct connection with agriculture now.

Football clubs almost all have some kind of familiar name or nickname, often also based on local tradition. Thus, Luton were known as 'The Hatters' because the local industry was millinery. The Ipswich Town nickname of recent years, 'The Tractor Boys', has been even more manufactured. Although it has been taken up with great alacrity by the British media, it was unheard of before the late 1990s. In the early days, as far back as the nineteenth century, the club was referred to as 'the Ipswich' and later on, for a considerable period of time 'the Blues' or simply 'Town' were used, as they still commonly are.

There appears to have been a period in the 1930s when some newspapers encouraged the use of a new sobriquet, 'the Witches'. At least one cartoon printed when Ipswich Town was election to the Football League showed the club's celebration being led by a friendly looking witch, but it doesn't seem to have ever caught on with supporters of the club. 'The Witches' is, of course, the name of the local speedway team to this day.

One explanation of the 'Tractor Boys' name is that, some years ago, Town fans used to shout 'Barrow Boys' at the supporters of opposing London clubs and that they sometimes would respond by shouting 'Tractor Boys' back. However, the most commonly accepted story is that the term was first used by Birmingham City fans as a taunt during Ipswich's first season back in the Premier League in the late 1990s, but caught on after the 2000/01 season after Town were promoted back to the Premier League and there was a great deal more coverage of the club in the media.

In an interview with the BBC in December 2000, Phil Ham, editor of Ipswich Town's longest-running and most successful fanzine and website, *Those Were the Days*, explained that it was a way of mocking Ipswich Town fans and their agricultural Suffolk roots:

> It's a long-term thing that has developed over the years really. Away fans have sung 'Ooo-arr, oooh-arr' but it was two years ago at Birmingham that things changed. We were being taunted, so we responded with 'one-nil to the Tractor Boys'. We may be rural country cousins but we *were* actually 1-0 up.

It appears that the Tractor Boys image appealed to the media more than it perhaps did to supporters, and Ipswich Town Football Club has itself exploited the name in its merchandising frequently since then. Even more recently, the media have referred to the club in turn as 'Roy Keane's Ipswich' and 'Paul Jewell's Ipswich', terminology that was as popular with supporters as the managers were.

Another concept that is now frequently used in the national media about Ipswich Town but is not based on any real tradition is the 'Old Farm Derby'. Commonly used to describe the rivalry between Ipswich Town and Norwich City, the phrase seems to have been more of a media invention than anything else, although the rivalry exists. There has even been a book with the title, *The Old Farm: Ipswich Town v. Norwich City: A History*, by Rob Hadgraft, published in 2005, which may have itself been responsible for popularising the use of the phrase. The rivalry between the clubs is genuine, but is probably neither as bitter or as long-standing as it may have been portrayed in recent times. Hadgraft, who is not a supporter of either side, claimed this dated back to the Suffolk-based Wuffingas (sixth to eighth century) and what the author calls the 'Icelingas' in the north of East Anglia. Whether he means the Iceni, which was a tribe of Britons in Roman times (*c.* first century BC to first century AD) or the Iclingas, a dynasty of the kings of Mercia, is unclear.

In reality, many Suffolk and Norfolk people have relatives either side of the border and it was not unusual in the past for supporters to watch both clubs. The animosity and aggression that came into football in the era of television coverage may have created a deeper rivalry, but it is fair to say that supporters of both clubs enjoy it to a greater or lesser extent, although it occasionally spills over into violence or vandalism. The name 'Old Farm' is certainly, I believe, entirely a media creation.

Ipswich Town has one connection with popular culture that makes it unique among English football clubs. Probably due to its high profile during the Robson era, several Ipswich Town players appeared in the 1981 film, *Escape to Victory*. The plot was based on a true story of the so-called 'Death Match', when FC Dynamo Kyiv played against and defeated a team of German soldiers in Ukraine when it was under Nazi occupation during the Second World War. The film was directed by John Huston and starred Sylvester Stallone and Michael Caine, but the abiding interest in it and, indeed, its cult status is due to the casting of a number of internationally known football stars, including Bobby Moore, Osvaldo Ardiles and Pelé. Several Ipswich Town players were also in the film, including John Wark (whose one line of dialogue had to be cut because of his impenetrable Glaswegian accent), Russell Osman, Laurie Sivell, Robin Turner and Kevin O'Callaghan. Others stood in for actors in the football scenes – Kevin Beattie played Michael Caine and Paul Cooper was Sylvester Stallone. Although its cult status is largely due to amusement at this rather bizarre concept, it's a testament to how famous Ipswich Town were under Bobby Robson's management that so many of his players were chosen to appear in it.

The importance of a club's image may mainly be seen in marketing terms by football administrators, but the way that Ipswich Town has been seen by others had always been important to the club and its supporters alike. The 'Ipswich Way' is an idea that it often held up as something to aspire to both on and off the pitch. In footballing terms, it means a certain way of playing football; a stylish passing game, which has only really occurred for brief periods in the club's history since 1878, and reached its apex when Bobby Robson was manager, making sporadic reappearances under George Burley and Jim Magilton. Supporters still hold to the tradition and – perhaps like all football fans – still place huge emphasis upon the style of football that they want to see played at Portman Road. Managers who don't understand this will usually have a short and unhappy stay at the club.

'The Ipswich Way' may be a woolly idea and most supporters would be hard-pressed to agree a definition of the term, but the concept lies dear to the hearts of most people involved with the club and a wise manager will embrace it even if he doesn't appreciate what it means to supporters. Paul Jewell made a great mistake in giving an interview to the local newspaper, the *East Anglian Daily Times* in October 2012, when he said:

> What is the Ipswich way? We have been in the Premier League for just five years of the last twenty-five. The traditions at this club are fantastic, it is very family-orientated and we should embrace that. But you can't forget the Ipswich way hasn't been very good over the last few years – since I have been here and before I was here. We want to try and play winning football, if that can be attractive then great. But our main aim at the minute is to get ourselves out of the hole we are in.

Even if Paul Jewell had been a good manager and had achieved more in his time at the club, rather than leaving it in danger of relegation back to the third division for the first time since the days of Ramsey, this short statement would have revealed to anyone who knows anything about Ipswich Town, that he was not the man for the job. His predecessor, Roy Keane – whose media image may have attracted the club's owner Marcus Evans to appoint him in the first place, but in reality overwhelmed the image of the club – also wanted to shake Ipswich Town up. As Nick Ames has written:

> Keane's perception, not an entirely unfair one, was that the squad contained too many nearly men, too many Alex Bruces and Owen Garvans – decent enough Championship footballers who wouldn't turn far from the middle of the road. Milling around these nearly men were too many familiar faces, too many old friends of the club popping in for a cup of tea, too many soft furnishings in a place that had never been ruled by decrees of steel. The noises were that to give Ipswich the hard edge required of a modern, promotion winning side, teeth might have to be pulled – but that, despite the pain, the perfect overbite that resulted would prove well worth it.

The image of Ipswich Town – and in particular of the Cobbold family – was probably created by the media. The Cobbolds were hugely popular with the press in their day, perhaps because of their undoubted generosity with alcoholic refreshments, and this in turn perpetuated the idea that, to use the now-clichéd words of chairman John Cobbold, there was only a crisis in the Ipswich Town Football Club boardroom when the white wine ran out. Perhaps even the 'Ipswich Way' itself may be artificial, but it has suited the supporters for many years, and it has only been questioned in recent times. Greater ruthlessness and commercialisation are seen as the only ways of bringing success back to the club in what is now perceived as the hard-bitten world of Premier League football, grasping players and greedy agents … although it depends on how success is defined.

There is little doubt that most people of Ipswich would love to return to a time, not that long ago, when in 2000 radio journalist, Pat Murphy, described it as being a place of 'good beer, good football and good people'. It may be a fantasy, it is almost certainly unrealistic, but what probably keeps the illusion alive so strongly is that it has been during the times when those very Ipswich Town traditions and values were at their strongest that the club has achieved its greatest glories.

15

George Burley

John Lyall officially resigned as manager of Ipswich Town Football Club on 5 December 1994, two days after the club went to the bottom of the Premier League following a defeat by Manchester City. Once again, the club's failings on the pitch had provoked protests by supporters. As a demonstration of the priorities of the 'football revolution', the press reports of events at Portman Road concentrated as much on the possibility of the club losing £5 million upon relegation as the failings of the football team.

George Burley had been a popular player for Ipswich Town, having been brought through the youth system. He had arrived at the age of seventeen, and played for Bobby Robson throughout the 'golden era', including in the 1978 FA Cup final and the UEFA Cup campaign of 1981; although he was to miss the final through injury. He was a popular choice for the new manager's job in 1994 too, but the appointment started badly because he had only recently taken up a similar job at nearby Colchester United. The prospect of returning to Ipswich was tempting for Burley, but because there was a disagreement or misunderstanding about the approach that the Suffolk club made, Colchester claimed that their new manager had been poached and sought compensation.

Burley, still only thirty-eight, resigned from the Colchester post on Christmas Eve 1994 to replace Paul Goddard, who had been the caretaker manager since the departure of John Lyall at the beginning of December. Goddard had expressed the desire to stay on, but as *The Times* described the club's season so far as 'severely challenged paddlewise up an increasingly muddy creek', his days were numbered. Burley would take over and become the last Ipswich Town manager to take the club back to the Premier League. He would also bring European football back to the club.

In 1994/95, however, the club was in too bad a state, both in footballing and financial terms, to be rescued immediately. George Burley could not prevent the club being relegated from the Premiership, and with it came the massive blow of losing the millions that now came with a place in the top flight.

David Sheepshanks, already on the Ipswich board, became chairman at the beginning of the 1995/96 season, and the relationship between him and the new manager may well have been key to the success that they would oversee together. Sheepshanks was a very different chairman to those that the club had known before. He was closely involved with the business side of running the club, and undoubtedly put in a tremendous amount of work. He also had a very high profile in the national media, partly because of his place at the Football Association – he was often mooted for the top job there during his time at Ipswich. Despite this, Sheepshanks always emphasised that he would be keeping to the Ipswich tradition of leaving football matters to the manager and his staff.

It was different with the business side, however. Sheepshanks was nothing if not ambitious for the club, but when he took over as chairman, he found it was in a parlous state financially; in his words, 'haemorrhaging to death'. He brought in local brewers Greene King as the main sponsors, and set about creating a more stable, commercially viable club, which he saw as a prerequisite for a long-term return to the Premier League.

The well-paid, high-profile players who had been responsible for Town's demise, such as Steve Sedgeley, David Linighan, Lee Chapman and Claus Thomsen, would leave over the next few years. Astutely, Burley would bring in his own players, including Tony Mowbray, who came from Celtic for £300,000 and would replace Linighan as club captain. Town would finish the 1995/96 season just outside the play-off places in seventh position. In the next four years they would be in contention for promotion by that route at the end of every season. Mowbray's experience and leadership would prove to be invaluable in the next few years, when every campaign would end with Ipswich battling for promotion in play-off matches that would eventually end with the prize of Premier League status at Wembley in May 2000.

Burley made a combination of clever transfer deals, bringing in two Dutch players, Gus Uhlenbeek (a former Ajax player, who came on trial from FC Oss and was signed for £100,000) and Bobby Petta (who came on a free transfer from Feyenoord), future captain Matt Holland from Bournemouth and Mark Venus from Wolves. He also had the luck to have several very talented players come through the Ipswich youth system at exactly the right time; James Scowcroft, Richard Wright and Kieron Dyer would all go on to become vitally important to Ipswich Town's success in that decade. Dyer was undoubtedly one of the finest young players of his time, and would have had a far more successful career for club and country had he not been plagued by injuries and illness.

In 1996/97, Town lost to Sheffield United on the away goals rule in the second leg of the play-off semi-final at Portman Road. They had led by two goals to nil after James Scowcroft and Niklas Gudmundsson scored. Although, according to the next day's *Daily Telegraph*, 'Ipswich dominated the second half, but laboured to take advantage of their superior amount of possession', the Blades went through following a seventy-sixth minute goal by their substitute, Walker.

The following season, it was the turn of Alan Curbishley's Charlton Athletic to beat Ipswich in the play-off semi-finals. After losing to Bolton Wanderers in a third successive play-off semi-final in 1999, Ipswich Town under George Burley were being branded by some people in the media as 'bottlers'. The defeat by Bolton (who would themselves lose in the final) was all the more galling because Town had only just missed automatic promotion by a single point.

Many fans became convinced that the only way that Ipswich Town would ever reach the Premiership again would be by winning the First Division outright, but they were proved wrong when the club was promoted in May 2000 after beating their old rivals, Bolton Wanderers, in the semi-finals, and then winning the play-off final against Barnsley at Wembley. It had been their fourth attempt in successive years.

Ipswich had again finished in third place in the League table and had an eventful 1999/2000 season, including beating their future play-off final opponents, Barnsey 6-1 at Portman Road in August 1999. Over previous seasons, having lost Dyer, Mathie, Taricco and Petta, Burley brought in other players who would all make an important contribution to the club's success: Jim Magilton, David Johnson, Jamie Clapham, Gary Croft, Richard Naylor and Martijn Reuser. In February 2000, Burley made what turned out to be an inspired acquisition by signing Marcus Stewart from Huddersfield Town for what seemed at the time to be the massive transfer fee of £2.5 million.

The play-off final in Wembley would be a wonderful way for the Ipswich faithful to see their club return to top-flight football, but before that they would see one of the most controversial and fiery encounters ever take place at Portman Road: the second leg of the play-off semi-final against Bolton Wanderers.

Having lost to Watford in the play-off final the year before, Sam Allardyce's Bolton were determined not to lose again. In the first leg at the Reebok Stadium, they had taken a 2-0 lead by half-time with goals by Dean Holdsworth and Eidur Gudjohnsen, but a brilliant recovery in stifling heat in the second half, and two superb goals by Marcus Stewart, meant that Ipswich went into their home leg with some confidence. With no advantage through away goals, Town still had to win the match.

Bolton took the lead in the sixth minute, but Ipswich equalised eleven minutes later. There was tension from the start, because it looked as if Town's goalkeeper, Richard Wright, had been fouled by Elliott. The Ipswich defenders had stopped playing, presumably because they were expecting Barry Knight to blow his whistle, but he didn't and Dean Holdsworth took advantage and put the ball in the net. The equaliser was from a penalty taken by Jim Magilton after Holdsworth had brought him down. Magilton visibly had to calm himself down, after what amounted to a brawl involving fifteen players followed the referee's decision to give a penalty.

Bolton went ahead again in the thirty-fifth minute, with another goal by Holdsworth, who placed it into the far corner beyond Richard Wright's reach. In the forty-fourth minute, Barry Knight awarded Ipswich a second penalty after Paul Ritchie had fouled Marcus Stewart. Again, the Bolton players surrounded the referee and appeared to verbally abuse him. It was a serious attempt to intimidate Knight, who wasn't even able to show the offenders a yellow card and at one point, he had to seek help from some stewards at the pitch side. Magilton went to take the penalty, but had to stop after Warhurst, one of the most aggressive of the Bolton side, said something to him during his run-up. On a second attempt, having clearly been taken under pressure, Magilton's penalty was saved by Jaaskelainen, who pushed it around the post.

The second half continued in the same vein, but town equalised in the forty-ninth minute when, as the *Daily Telegraph* report put it, Magilton 'evaded a challenge from Whitlow, ghosted past Warhurst and Ritchie and drove a magnificent half volley beyond Jaaskelainen'. Bolton regained their lead, however, with a volley by Johnston from over 30 yards away from the goal.

Magilton, who was having a magnificent game, again scored an equaliser, this one in the ninetieth minute of normal time. Soon afterwards, Whitlow was sent off for a professional foul. In extra time, Jamie Clapham scored Ipswich's third goal of the match from the penalty spot. By this time, the Bolton men's frustration had got the better of them, and they were further reduced after Robbie Elliott was sent off. Martijn Reuser put the final nail in their coffin with a superb strike in the 109th minute.

In that highly charged atmosphere, the referee, Barry Knight, had issued Bolton players with a total of ten yellow cards and sent two of them, Mike Whitlow and Robbie Elliott, off. The final score was 5-3 to Ipswich and they went through to the Wembley final on an aggregate score of 7-5.

The atmosphere at Wembley Stadium on 29 May 2000 was completely different. It would be the last play-off game at the old Wembley before it was rebuilt, and 73,427 Ipswich Town and Barnsey supporters brought a festive atmosphere with them. It was an emotional day for David

Sheepshanks, George Burley and perhaps especially for Keiron Dyer, who was watching the game from the stands. He had wept when his hometown side had lost their chance of promotion the previous season, knowing that he would have to leave the club. Having beaten Barnsley twice in the League that season, Ipswich should have been confident, but it was a game where each side's fortunes changed throughout, and it was only in the eighty-third minute, when Hristov failed to score for Barnsley, that Town supporters felt that they could win.

After losing David Johnson early in the game, Ipswich conceded the first goal, following a dubious decision by referee Terry Heilbron who was officiating in his last game. Richard Wright almost reached Craig Hignett's shot, but the ball hit the crossbar, bounced out and rebounded off his back into the net.

It was an inauspicious start. Wright would make amends by saving a Darren Barnard penalty just before half-time, but only after Tony Mowbray had equalised with a 'textbook header' in the twenty-eighth minute. In the second half, Ipswich quickly took the lead after Richard Naylor controlled a ball knocked down by Marcus Stewart. Naylor, who spent most of his career as a defender, but had come on as a substitute to replace Johnson and had what must have been one of the games of his life, kept his head and scored. He was booked for taking his shirt off in celebration. After that point, Ipswich were the dominant side and Marcus Stewart made it 3-1 in the fifty-ninth minute by superbly heading Clapham's cross past Barnsley goalkeeper, Miller. The game should have been over, but yet another penalty was awarded against Town when Mowbray fouled Geoff Thomas. Hignett took the penalty and scored making for a nervous last half-hour, in which Barnsley constantly pressed for an equaliser. Shortly after Wright had brilliantly saved Hristov's point blank shot on his goal, Burley sent Martijn Reuser on as a substitute. In stoppage time, Ipswich broke from a well-placed pass by Richard Naylor, and Reuser ran 40 yards before lifting the ball over Miller and into the goal. One television commentator simply uttered the words: 'Reuser – Premiership' – they were words that defined the moment for many fans. Ipswich Town were back in the top flight at last.

Ipswich Town were to stay in the Premier League for only two years. In the first season, they excelled themselves, and exceeded all expectations by finishing the season in fifth place behind Manchester United, Arsenal, Liverpool and Leeds United. They were doubtless assisted by the magnificent form of Marcus Stewart, who scored twenty-one goals and rivalled Thierry Henry for the title of top goalscorer.

As a result, Ipswich qualified for the UEFA Cup, and in many ways became the victims of their own success. The club felt under pressure to 'improve' what was a cohesive and effective young squad by bringing in expensive new players who failed to deliver. David Sheepshanks also committed the club to the expense of building a new stand. What followed was relegation back to the second tier, something from which Ipswich have never recovered, and serious financial problems leaving the club with massive debts. Burley was sacked and replaced by Joe Royle, who consolidated the team and made a good attempt at taking them back to the Premiership, particularly given the financial constraints he was under. Some of the best players like Matt Holland and Hermann Hreidarsson had to leave. Once again, it was the club's inability to compete in the commercial world that affected its chances as much as what happened on the football field.

Marcus Evans, a reclusive but very wealthy businessman, bought a majority share in the club in 2007 and David Sheepshanks moved on to take a role in the development of the Football Association's national football centre, St George's. Since then, the club has moved further than ever away from its tradition of giving managers time to build a side. Jim Magilton, Roy Keane and Paul Jewell have all been given a chance, but Ipswich has ended each season lower down the division. Since the arrival of Mick McCarthy as manager, the club's fortunes seem to have improved and its owner, Marcus Evans, has publicly reiterated his desire to take the club back to its halycon days as one of the best-loved football clubs in Europe.

Sources

Books

Brittain, Vera, *Testament of Youth* (Gollancz, 1939)

Cullum, Sir John, *The History and Antiquities of Hawsted in the County of Suffolk*. 2nd ed. (J. Nichols, 1813)

Eastwood, John & Tony Moyse, *The Men Who Made The Town* (Almeida Books, 1986)

Glyde, John, *The Moral, Social & Religious History of Ipswich in the Middle of the Nineteenth Century* (J. M. Burton & Co., 1850)

Grace, Frank, *Rags and Bones; a social history of a working-class community in nineteenth-century Ipswich* (Unicorn, 2005)

Graves, Robert & Alan Hodge, *The Long Week-end: a social history of Great Britain, 1918-1939* (Macmillan, 1941)

Gray, I. E. & W. E. Potter, *Ipswich School, 1400–1950* (Harrison, 1950)

Hadgraft, Rob, *The Old Farm: Ipswich Town v Norwich City: A History* (Desert Island Books, 2005)

Henderson, Mel & Paul Voller, *The Essential History of Ipswich Town*, (Headline, 2001)

Inglis, Simon, *Football Grounds of Britain*. 3rd ed. (Collins Willow, 1996)

Kelly's Post Office Directory of Suffolk for 1865

Malster, Robert, *A History of Ipswich* (Phillimore, 2000)

Marquis, Max, *Anatomy of a Football Manager: Alf Ramsey* (Arthur Barker, 1970)

Rice, Ken, *Ipswich: an Illustrated History of Ipswich Town* (Wensum Books, 1973)

Taylor, Rogan, *Football and Its Fans: supporters and their relations with the game, 1885–1985* (Leicester University Press, 1992)

Tusser, Thomas, *Five Hundreth Pointes of Good Husbandrie* (1573; reprinted by Oxford University Press, 1984)

Walvin, James, *The People's Game*. 2nd revised ed. (Mainstream, 1994)

Newspapers
The following newspapers (between 1870 and 1960) were viewed either on the British Newspaper Archive [http://www.britishnewspaperarchive. co.uk/] or the Gale [www.galegroup.com] websites:

The Times, Daily Express, Daily Mirror, Daily Sketch, Daily Telegraph, Derby Daily Telegraph, Evening Star, East Anglian Daily Times, Essex Chronicle, Ipswich Journal, Sheffield Daily Telegraph, Sunday Mirror, Sunday Pictorial, Western Daily Press – online archives via either [website] or British Newspaper Archive [website]

Fanzines
Those Were The Days
Turnstile Blues

Internet-Based Sources
Pride of Anglia: [http://www.tmwmtt.com/poa/index.html]
Ipswich Town on the ball with new stand by Susan Dawson in *Architect's Journal*, 2003: [http://www.architectsjournal.co.uk/home/ipswich-town-on-the-ball-with-new-stand/147552.article]
Roy Keane's 7.5 Million Fatal Flaws by Nick Ames [http://lastseatontheplane.wordpress.com/2011/01/07/roy-keanes-7-5-million-fatal-flaws/]
Architect's Journal [http://www.architectsjournal.co.uk/home/ipswich-town-on-the-ball-with-new-stand/147552.article]

Other Media
Boys of '81: Ipswich Town [DVD] (Vision Sport, 2007)
Desert Island Discs: Interview with Bobby Robson by Michael Parkinson (BBC, 1986)

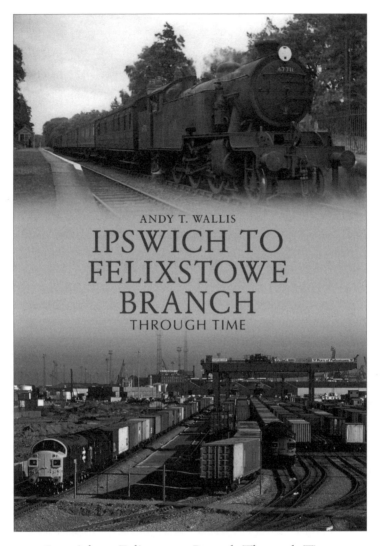

Ipswich to Felixstowe Branch Through Time

Andy T. Wallis

This fascinating selection of photographs traces some of the many ways in which the Ipswich to Felixstowe Branch has changed and developed over the last century.

978 1 4456 0766 5

96 pages, full colour

MICHAEL ROUSE

FELIXSTOWE

THROUGH TIME

Felixstowe Through Time
Michael Rouse

This fascinating selection of photographs traces some of the many
ways in which Felixstowe has changed and developed over the last
century.

978 1 4456 1086 3
96 pages, full colour

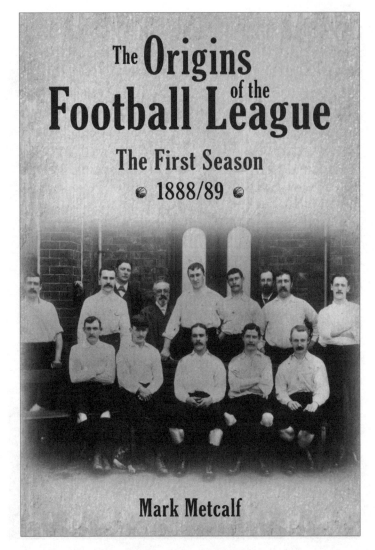

The Origins of the Football League
Mark Metcalf

Who scored the first-ever League goal? Find out the definitive
answer in *The Origins of the Football League*. For the first time, the
history of the Football League's first season is told in great depth,
with reports on every match and profiles of all those who played.

978 1 4456 1881 4
224 pages, including 32 b&w images

Available from all good bookshops or order direct
from our website www.amberleybooks.com